W9-CKI-259

11/10

GLOBALVIEWPOINTS

| The Internet

Other Books of Related Interest:

Current Controversies Series

Should the Internet Be Free?

Global Viewpoints

Freedom of Expression

Introducing Issues with Opposing Viewpoints Series

Globalization

Issues on Trial

Cybercrime

Free Speech

Intellectual Property Rights

Issues That Concern You

Downloading Music

Internet Safety

Intellectual Property Rights

Opposing Viewpoints Series

Censorship

Civil Liberties

Copyright Infringement

Globalization

GLOBALVIEWPOINTS

The Internet

Gary Wiener, Book Editor

GREENHAVEN PRESS
A part of Gale, Cengage Learning

GALE
CENGAGE Learning™

Detroit • New York • San Francisco • New Haven, Conn • Waterville, Maine • London

Christine Nasso, *Publisher*
Elizabeth Des Chenes, *Managing Editor*

© 2010 Greenhaven Press, a part of Gale, Cengage Learning

For more information, contact:
Greenhaven Press
27500 Drake Rd.
Farmington Hills, MI 48331-3535
Or you can visit our Internet site at gale.cengage.com

For product information and technology assistance, contact us at

Gale Customer Support, 1-800-877-4253
For permission to use material from this text or product, submit all requests online at
www.cengage.com/permissions

Further permissions questions can be emailed to permissionrequest@cengage.com

Articles in Greenhaven Press anthologies are often edited for length to meet page requirements. In addition, original titles of these works are changed to clearly present the main thesis and to explicitly indicate the author's opinion. Every effort is made to ensure that Greenhaven Press accurately reflects the original intent of the authors. Every effort has been made to trace the owners of copyrighted material.

Cover image © Frederic Soltan/Sygma/Corbis.

LIBRARY OF CONGRESS CATALOGING-IN-PUBLICATION DATA

The internet / Gary Wiener, book editor.
    p. cm. -- (Global viewpoints)
    Includes bibliographical references and index.
    ISBN 978-0-7377-4935-9 (hardcover) -- ISBN 978-0-7377-4936-6 (pbk.)
    1. Internet--Social aspects--Juvenile literature. 2. Internet--Political aspects--Juvenile literature. 3. Computer crimes--Juvenile literature. I. Wiener, Gary.
    HM851.I56958 2010
    303.48'33--dc22
                                                                2010005978

Printed in the United States of America
1 2 3 4 5 6 7 14 13 12 11 10

Contents

Chapter 2: The Political Impact of the Internet

Chapter 3: Internet Regulation and Censorship

Chapter 4: Cybercrime and Cyberwar

Foreword

"The problems of all of humanity can
only be solved by all of humanity."
—Swiss author Friedrich Dürrenmatt

Global interdependence has become an undeniable reality. Mass media and technology have increased worldwide access to information and created a society of global citizens. Understanding and navigating this global community is a challenge, requiring a high degree of information literacy and a new level of learning sophistication.

Building on the success of its flagship series, *Opposing Viewpoints*, Greenhaven Press has created the *Global Viewpoints* series to examine a broad range of current, often controversial topics of worldwide importance from a variety of international perspectives. Providing students and other readers with the information they need to explore global connections and think critically about worldwide implications, each *Global Viewpoints* volume offers a panoramic view of a topic of widespread significance.

Drugs, famine, immigration—a broad, international treatment is essential to do justice to social, environmental, health, and political issues such as these. Junior high, high school, and early college students, as well as general readers, can all use *Global Viewpoints* anthologies to discern the complexities relating to each issue. Readers will be able to examine unique national perspectives while, at the same time, appreciating the interconnectedness that global priorities bring to all nations and cultures.

Material in each volume is selected from a diverse range of sources, including journals, magazines, newspapers, nonfiction books, speeches, government documents, pamphlets, organization newsletters, and position papers. *Global Viewpoints* is truly global, with material drawn primarily from international sources available in English and secondarily from U.S. sources with extensive international coverage.

Features of each volume in the *Global Viewpoints* series include:

- An **annotated table of contents** that provides a brief summary of each essay in the volume, including the name of the country or area covered in the essay.

- An **introduction** specific to the volume topic.

- A **world map** to help readers locate the countries or areas covered in the essays.

- For each viewpoint, an **introduction** that contains notes about the author and source of the viewpoint explains why material from the specific country is being presented, summarizes the main points of the viewpoint, and offers three **guided reading questions** to aid in understanding and comprehension.

- **For further discussion** questions that promote critical thinking by asking the reader to compare and contrast aspects of the viewpoints or draw conclusions about perspectives and arguments.

- A worldwide list of **organizations to contact** for readers seeking additional information.

- A **periodical bibliography** for each chapter and a **bibliography of books** on the volume topic to aid in further research.

- A comprehensive **subject index** to offer access to people, places, events, and subjects cited in the text, with the countries covered in the viewpoints highlighted.

Global Viewpoints is designed for a broad spectrum of readers who want to learn more about current events, history, political science, government, international relations, economics, environmental science, world cultures, and sociology—students doing research for class assignments or debates, teachers and faculty seeking to supplement course materials, and others wanting to understand current issues better. By presenting how people in various countries perceive the root causes, current consequences, and proposed solutions to worldwide challenges, *Global Viewpoints* volumes offer readers opportunities to enhance their global awareness and their knowledge of cultures worldwide.

Introduction

> *"Twenty years ago no one could have imagined the effects the Internet would have: entire relationships flourish, friendships prosper . . . there's a vast new intimacy and accidental poetry. . . . The entire human experience seems to unveil itself like the surface of a new planet."*
>
> *—English writer J.G. Ballard*

In a December 2009 opinion piece, syndicated columnist Kevin Horrigan suggested the radical change in society wrought by the Internet. He wondered what would happen in the twenty-first century if an eight-year-old girl asked her father if there were a Santa Claus. A century earlier, that scenario occasioned the famous editorial column, "Yes, Virginia, There Is a Santa Claus" in the now-defunct *New York Sun* newspaper. In present day, Horrigan wrote, Virginia O'Hanlon would probably Google "Santa" and "exist," only to come across a *Spy* magazine article "that explains that the laws of physics would cause reindeer to vaporize if they attempted to fly fast enough to visit all of the children in the world." The *Spy* magazine article concluded that Santa would be crushed by the G-forces. Horrigan concluded that Virginia would be crushed by the news.

This scenario sums up everything that is right and wrong about the Internet in the early twenty-first century: One may find information on virtually any subject, yet there is almost too much information out there and much of it is suspect. As one oncologist, Dr. Jeffrey Raizer, suggested on December 24, 2009, when interviewed on the *Bonnie Hunt Show*, everyone has access to a world of information about illnesses on the Internet, but "it gives everybody more information" about a given disease "than I think most people would even care to know about."

Given the Internet's virtual ubiquity in contemporary world, it is hard for many people to imagine life without it. In the twenty-first century, many people pay their bills online; they plan trips using mapping Web sites; they interact with friends they haven't actually seen in years. In light of all this, it is easy to forget that the Internet has only become a viable communications tool in the last two decades. There was no Internet as we now know it until the mid-1990s, when service providers such as America Online (AOL), Prodigy, and CompuServe allowed ordinary people to access the World Wide Web.

Jokes about Al Gore's supposed claim that he invented the Internet aside, the Internet really was the brainchild of the U.S. government, as a military response to the Soviet Union's launch of Sputnik in 1957. Not to be confused with the World Wide Web, the Internet is the hardware and software network that allows computers to connect with one another, while the Web is composed of all of the interconnected documents. During the Cold War between the Soviet Union and the United States in the 1960s, the U.S. Department of Defense needed a system to link supercomputers, so that if one or more were destroyed in a nuclear attack, others would still be able to communicate. The first such system, connected in the late 1960s, was called ARPANET (Advanced Research Projects Agency Network), and linked computers from four western universities: the University of California, Los Angeles (UCLA); the University of California, Santa Barbara; the University of Utah; and Stanford University. This system was not for the general public, however: It was used mainly by academics, scientists, and engineers.

Over the next decade, as universities saw the promise of ARPANET, other networks such as UUCP and Usenet began to emerge. But these networks were isolated from each other. In order to connect information from these various networks, new protocols, or rules that computers use to send information, had to be devised. In the early 1980s, scientists invented TCP/IP (Transmission Control Protocol/Internet Protocol) to regulate information from the various networks and to ensure that information reaches the proper destination. In 1982, various networks began to connect with each other, and the term "Internet" was coined.

The great breakthrough in facilitating ordinary citizens' Internet participation came with the invention of the World Wide Web in the early 1990s. A scientist named Tim Berners-Lee, working for a high-energy physics lab in Switzerland, developed software with hypermedia capabilities. From Berners-Lee's early design, the hyperlink—so necessary to the success of the Internet and so omnipresent in today's online experience—was born. It was at this point that the Internet exploded. In 1993, there were little more than one hundred Web sites. A year later, there were more than 2,700. By 1995, the figure reached 23,500. Now, there are hundreds of millions.

Many observers have tried to pin down exactly what it is about the Internet that has revolutionized modern life. Some make the claim for its amazing ability to connect people from all different walks of life and from countries around the world. Additionally, there is the means to not just communicate with those in distant locales, but to communicate instantly and freely via applications such as chat, e-mail, and VoIP (voice over Internet protocol). Others celebrate the Internet's storehouse of knowledge, which enables anyone to access a massive amount of information previously only available in thousands of libraries worldwide. In his book about viral culture, *And Then There's This: How Stories Live and Die in Viral Culture*, Bill Wasik notes the following benefit of the Internet: "What the Internet has done to change culture—is to *archive* trillions of our communications, to make them linkable, trackable, searchable, quantifiable, so that they can serve as ready grist for more conversation." The Internet is, as Wasik claims, not just a new way to communicate, but a new way to measure and interpret how we communicate.

With any gift as great as that of the Internet, abuses are sure to follow. The Internet has enabled those who prey on others in the real world—child pornographers, con men, thieves, and counterfeiters among them—to thrive in the on-line world. Many have tried to place the blame on the Internet itself for enabling such evils, but this raises a thorny issue: Is the Internet itself promoting such behavior, or is it simply a vehicle for behavior that would take place off-line if there were no World Wide Web? For example, online gambling, fueled by the publicity given to Texas Hold'em poker by the traditional media, is certain to become a twenty-first century dilemma. But if there were no Internet, would gambling addicts find another outlet to pursue their passion? And what of those addicted to the Internet itself, those who spend hour upon hour surfing the Web? Is the Internet responsible for this behavior, or would addicts simply find off-line alternatives if there were no Internet? Such questions will undoubtedly be the subject of numerous studies going forward.

Besides facilitating addictive activities, the Internet has provided a vehicle for all types of criminal endeavors. Con men bombard the gullible with advertisements aimed at bilking their victims out of large sums of money. Governments such as North Korea attack other countries by shutting down their services. Terrorist organizations use the Web to plot and plan activities, to boast of successes, and to recruit new members. According to journalist Zeeshan Aleem, "Many jihadists-to-be are exposed to the people and the ideas that radicalize them through the Internet. . . . Indeed, the Internet allows for the mobilization of terrorist-inclined youth to an extent [that would] not otherwise be possible." In order to give labels to the Internet's facilitation of such destructive activities, "cybercrime," "cyberwarfare" and "cyberterrorism," terms not even imagined by the public in those early days of the 1990s, have now come into common vocabulary.

There are more subtle negatives to be found in Internet culture, some claim. With so-called Web 2.0 came the ability of users not merely to read what others have put online, but to establish their own presence. Now, anyone with an opinion can post claims for all to read—claims that are often doubtful at best, and at worst, completely incorrect. Wikipedia, the online encyclopedia that depends on user-generated content, is a prime example of this tendency. While most of the information Wikipedia contains is verifiably correct, users can post incorrect information, propaganda, advertisements posing as facts, and other distortions of the truth. This unreliability factor is, of course, true everywhere on the Internet. Users must be discriminating in how they use Internet information and what they believe. This notion is suggested in the now-famous *New Yorker* cartoon in which one hound, sitting at a computer, says to another, "On the Internet no one knows you're a dog." While proponents have celebrated the democratizing characteristics of the Internet that allow anyone to post any thought at any time, detractors have bemoaned the same freedoms. In his diatribe against the Internet, *The Cult of the Amateur: How Today's Internet Is Killing Our Culture*, Andrew Keen observes that the plethora of ignorant opinions available on the Internet is drowning out the wiser, more thoughtful voices. Keen characterizes the contemporary Internet as "ignorance meets egoism meets bad taste meets mob rule . . . on steroids."

As more and more traditional media found an online presence in the late twentieth and early twenty-first centuries, Internet controversies grew exponentially. Google began to scan print media, especially books, and place such content online, raising central issues about content ownership; China censored online activity, leading some to dub their efforts the

"Great Firewall of China"; Google's satellite pictures of every conceivable place on Earth led some to question their all-seeing cameras as a violation of privacy; Craigslist, the Internet classified advertisement site, has enabled sex workers to proffer their trade via the Web.

The Internet has clearly changed life as we know it, and only one thing is certain: It will continue to have an impact on the way more and more people worldwide go about their daily lives. *Global Viewpoints: The Internet* explores this modern-day medium from a number of different perspectives: the cultural impact of the Internet, the political impact of the Internet, Internet regulation and censorship, and the dangers of cyberwar and cyberterrorism. This volume presents a wide-ranging collection of viewpoints that celebrate a great invention and its myriad uses, as well as those that urge caution and counsel users to navigate insightfully through the maze that is the World Wide Web.

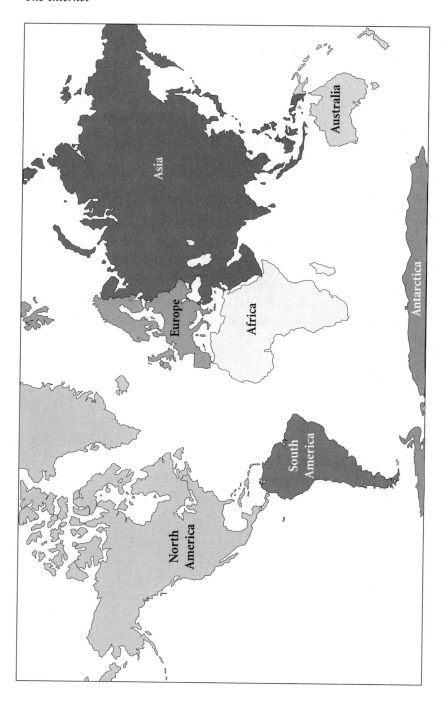

**GLOBAL**VIEWPOINTS

C HAPTER 1

The Cultural Impact
of the Internet

The Internet Makes Distance Matter Less for Good and Ill

Barry S. Fagin

In the following excerpted viewpoint, Barry S. Fagin argues that both opportunities and challenges come together with new technology. The invention of the Internet surpasses other technological discoveries because it has affected so many people in so short a time. Benefits of the Internet include the ability to virtually visit places one cannot get to physically, keeping in touch with friends and family via e-mail and webcam technology, enhanced participation in politics, and the growth of freedom. Challenges include information overload, the exploitation of people, especially children, through online pornography, and increased vulnerability to attack by one's enemies.

Barry S. Fagin is professor of computer science, a senior fellow in technology policy at Colorado's Independence Institute, and cofounder of Families Against Internet Censorship.

As you read, consider the following questions:

1. According to Fagin, what major technological advances does the invention of the Internet surpass?
2. According to the article, how does the Internet promote the growth of freedom?
3. According to Fagin, what kinds of groups can use the Internet to attack the United States?

Barry S. Fagin, "Intellectual Freedom and Social Responsibility: As We Grow More Dependent on the Internet, We Grow More Vulnerable," *World & I*, vol. 17, no. 3, March 2002, pp. 38ff. Copyright © 2002 News World Communications, Inc.

Any new technology brings opportunities and challenges. The taming of fire, the invention of the printing press, and the discovery of DNA were all major technological events that stretched our thinking. They forced us to reexamine how society should be organized, how we should live our lives, and even what it means to be human. Changes and social upheaval wrought by the Internet should be seen as part of that recurring theme. The creations of man's mind have always stirred the fires of his heart.

The Internet, however, is unique in its breadth and depth: Nothing in the history of civilization has affected so many people in so short a time. If the job of scientists is to make philosophers' lives difficult, then the Internet may be our greatest success. Let's see why.

The Benefits

The possibility of information access from anywhere at any time means that distance isn't as important as it once was. This empowers individuals: In a world where distance matters less, people matter more.

Most people cannot travel to Paris to see the Louvre: www .louvre.fr brings the museum to them. You may live in a place that doesn't have a world-class university, but you can download course materials from www.mit.edu. You may not know anyone who has to care for a spouse with Alzheimer's, but you can find hundreds of them online who will answer questions and provide emotional support.

I'm typing this article from across the ocean, but a voice/ Webcam chat with my family is a mouse click away. These are all examples of how the Internet reduces the importance of distance.

Additionally, citizens in democratic regimes benefit from easy access to information the Internet provides. Democracy works best when its citizens are informed, its elections fair, and its leaders accountable.

The Internet has produced social benefits in all these areas. In the United States, virtually all candidates for national, state, and in many cases local office have Web sites to acquaint prospective voters with their positions. Most members of Congress also have Web sites and regularly use email to communicate with their constituents. Government agencies publish forms and searchable databases online, making it easier for citizens to get their questions answered.

The Internet confronts authoritarian regimes with an impossible choice: how to obtain the economic benefits of the Internet for citizens, while still controlling their access to information.

Many state governments have Web sites where visitors can track legislation, examine voting records, and review transcripts of committee meetings. (My home state of Colorado has an excellent Web site.) Overseas, sites like Russia's www.elections.ru can help fledgling democracies take root and grow as first-time voters come online to learn about candidates and political parties.

For countries enjoying the benefits of freedom and democracy, embracing the Internet has been relatively painless. For other nations, the process has proved more difficult. The Internet confronts authoritarian regimes with an impossible choice: how to obtain the economic benefits of the Internet for citizens, while still controlling their access to information.

This choice is impossible because the laws of physics do not distinguish between bits that represent investment capital and bits that represent ideas. Such distinctions are made only in the human mind.

Confronting this dilemma has caused many authoritarian nations to relax their policies of information control, in a tacit acknowledgment that the Internet renders separating freedom of information from economic growth impossible. Jordan, Egypt, Morocco, Malaysia, and Singapore fall into this category.

Other countries, sadly, have gone the other way. Iraq, Libya, and North Korea have no Internet connections, virtually guaranteeing their continued economic stagnation and isolation from the rest of the world.

A few nations, notably China and Saudi Arabia, still want it both ways. They are trying to develop an Internet infrastructure while at the same time implementing some of the most repressive Internet regulation regimes in the world. Internet service providers (ISPs) are either owned directly by the state or are held responsible for blocking content in many categories. Internet cafés in these countries are required to run programs that block access to banned Web sites, record chat room conversations, and notify authorities of suspicious activity.

In the end, these attempts will prove unsuccessful. Cheap cell phones, free encryption technology, universal email, and international Web sites are already being used to circumvent Internet content laws. Such laws will become even less relevant as the technology gets better and cheaper.

China, Saudi Arabia, and other nations seeking a middle way for the Internet must eventually realize there is none. At that point, the Internet will have become so interwoven in the fabric of their economic life that cutting off access will not be possible. De facto freedom of information will slowly emerge in these countries, even if never officially recognized. This will be one of the Internet's most significant contributions to global civilization.

The Costs

The same things that make the Internet such a strong force for improvement of the human condition also present great challenges. The availability of instant information, anytime and anywhere, can exploit many areas of human weakness, presenting significant challenges to how we relate to one another. The free flow of information may show flagrant disregard for intellectual property: The same economic system of law and property rights that gave birth to the Internet is now potentially threatened by it.

Until society has adjusted to the availability of enormous amounts of information on a nonstop basis, the Internet has a strong potential to adversely affect social relationships. Individuals can spend inordinate amounts of time online simply trying to manage all the information that they encounter. Sociologists warn of information overload as we confront the totality of mankind's stored knowledge whenever we go online.

Science fiction authors have often speculated about experience machines, which allow users to experience anything they wish. The Internet is not quite an experience machine, but nothing before it has ever come close.

Just as some people can drink socially while others are extremely vulnerable to alcohol addiction, so too can people be affected in different ways by the online experience. In its extreme form, it resembles addiction.

Lonely, bored, or unsupervised teenagers can spend hours in online chat rooms, where they are vulnerable to exploitation and predation. Disaffected, pathological individuals can use the Internet to socialize exclusively with others like themselves, reinforcing their own (often hate-filled) worldviews and contributing to social unrest.

The dramatically increased availability of sexually explicit material online is a part of this picture. Internet pornography, now a multibillion-dollar industry and one of the first profitable sectors of the Internet economy, becomes a problem when it involves children or is viewed in a public setting.

One study estimates that 20 percent of all white-collar males access pornography online while at work. A maker of Web-monitoring software claims that pornography and other nonwork-related Web access during work hours cost over \$50 billion in lost productivity. Clearly, this is a serious problem.

Finally, as we grow more dependent on the Internet, we grow more vulnerable. Before the Internet, viruses could be spread from one computer to another only through floppy disks. With the widespread availability of software downloaded from Web sites or distributed through email, viruses now spread like wildfire, covering the world in hours.

The same standards that promote ease of information exchange can be exploited by virus writers. Some of the most virulent programs ever written exploit features designed to make computers easier to use. Being able to double-click on attachments in an email message is very convenient, until it erases your hard disk.

The same factors that empower legitimate Internet users also empower those opposed to our national interests. There is no escaping this fundamental fact.

These problems will only get worse with the widespread adoption of broadband, in which users are connected through a high-bandwidth channel 24 hours a day. Hostile sweeper programs can take advantage of this by probing computers connected to the Internet for vulnerabilities.

Internet-related vulnerabilities affect not just our economy but our national security. Hostile countries too weak to attack the United States militarily can still strike at our Internet infrastructure from within the safety of their own borders. Even countries that bear no military grudge toward the United States are eager for our technology. The Internet provides them with an unprecedented opportunity to devote national resources toward industrial espionage.

Internationally outlawed groups that lack the budget of a nation-state can use the Internet against America. With so much of our public life now available online, terrorists no longer need to risk coming here to gather information before an attack, nor do they need to meet in person to communicate. The same factors that empower legitimate Internet users also empower those opposed to our national interests. There is no escaping this fundamental fact. . . .

The Internet Is Destroying the World

A.N. Wilson

A.N. Wilson argues in the following viewpoint that the Internet is changing the world for the worse. Formerly a believer in the wonder of the Internet, Wilson was convinced otherwise by comments from Google executive Eric Schmidt and author Andrew Keen's exposé on the potential evils of the Internet. Wilson believes that the Internet is blurring the lines between fiction and truth, creating a generation of gambling and pornography addicts, and putting legitimate companies out of business through illegal downloading of intellectual property. He forecasts a grim future, a hellish climate where every Internet move will be recorded, and from which Internet surfers will have no escape.

Wilson is a writer known for his critical biographies, novels, and works of popular and cultural history. He is also a columnist for the London Evening Standard *and has written for the* Daily Mail, *the* Times Literary Supplement, New Statesman, *the* Spectator *magazine, and the* Observer.

As you read, consider the following questions:

1. What is A.N. Wilson's definition of Web 2.0 in this viewpoint?
2. What company was behind the *Tea Party* video?

3. According to the viewpoint, how far did the Disney company's sales fall between 2003 and 2005?

Your child is next door on the computer, destroying the world as we know it and wrecking two of the most fundamental values that underpin society—first, as I shall explain, the distinction between truth and falsehood; second, the inviolability of personal property.

While the little blighter is about it, your darling ten-year-old is also helping to destroy the record industry, the publishing industry, newspapers and cinema. And what is more, this activity is highly addictive and is more likely than not to make young people into addicts of gambling, pornography and insidious forms of self-deception.

Maybe you think that is an exaggerated reaction to watching a young person slump down in front of the laptop with that intensity of concentration which is seldom, if ever, shown during actual live conversation?

Your darling ten-year-old is . . . helping to destroy the record industry, the publishing industry, newspapers and cinema. And . . . this activity is highly addictive.

Until recently, I too would have thought it absurd to voice such fears about the marvellous technological revolution which has come to us, not just since the invention of the Internet, but even more recently, by the enhancement that is called Web 2.0.

Web 2.0 Creates Opportunity as Well as Danger

For those unfamiliar with such terms, Web 2.0 is the name given by the computer industry to the "second generation" of the Internet that has now been made widely available and affordable by high-speed broadband connections.

Such is the capability of Web 2.0 that it makes all kinds of information available instantaneously at the click of a mouse, and enables entire books, films and albums to be downloaded to your desktop.

It can be a wonderful thing to use. I have myself been seduced by the ease, and the interest, of using Google and Wikipedia (the popular online encyclopaedia) to check facts in seconds which would formerly have required a wearisome journey to a library or would simply have been inaccessible. Nothing wrong with that, surely?

And isn't it simply fuddy-duddy to say that young people should not have access to an enormous range of knowledge and experience at the tap of a laptop key, or to build up friendships through "social networking" sites such as Facebook, Bebo and MySpace?

Until recently, I would certainly have agreed [with] Web evangelists: Let Freedom Reign! Yes, there may be a lot of drivel out there, but, with judicious parental supervision, surely the world of the Internet creates untold opportunities for everyone—including our children—to inform, entertain and delight themselves.

Yet two things have made me change my mind. The first was the speech given recently by Eric Schmidt, Google's chief executive, in which he outlined the company's plans for the future.

Not content with becoming the world's dominant Internet search engine, he revealed that Google hoped to acquire a mass of personal information about each of its regular users, to the extent that it will one day be able to tell people how they should conduct almost every aspect of their lives.

"The goal is to enable Google users to be able to ask questions such as 'What shall I do tomorrow?' and 'What job shall I take?'" said Mr Schmidt.

For anyone who cares about personal liberties and privacy, this is a truly terrifying prospect. But if you think that, then you should also read—as I did this week—a staggering new book with the title *The Cult of the Amateur: How Today's Internet Is Killing Our Culture* by Andrew Keen.

The goal is to enable Google users to be able to ask questions such as 'What shall I do tomorrow?' and 'What job shall I take?'

He is an English-born digital media entrepreneur and Silicon Valley insider who really knows his stuff. And he writes with the passion of a man who can at last see the dangers he has helped unleash.

His book will come as a real shock to many. It certainly did to me.

The Blurring of Truth

Let us concentrate first on Keen's assertion that the innocent use of the World Wide Web as a source of knowledge has blurred any distinction between truth and falsehood.

Wikipedia was started by a clever man called Jimmy Wales. I have often used it, being too lazy even to tap the few extra digits to read a proper online encyclopaedia such as the *Encyclopaedia Britannica*. I had never realized until reading Keen's book that any amateur can write an entry in Wikipedia.

What is more, if you don't like an entry, you can "correct" it, whether what you write is true or false. As a result, Wikipedia is now insidiously crammed with misinformation, much of it planted by special interest groups or malign individuals with axes to grind.

Yet it is also the 17th most accessed site on the Internet. *Encyclopaedia Britannica*, with 100 Nobel Prize winners, 4,000 expert contributors, and its strict code of accuracy and objectivity, is ranked 5,128.

The result? Error-crammed and often biased Wikipedia, which pays for none of its contributions and employs only a handful of staff, is going from strength to strength. Meanwhile, *Britannica* has had to halve its 300 or so staff in the U.S.

[Wikipedia is] the 17th most accessed site on the Internet. Encyclopaedia Britannica, *with 100 Nobel Prize winners, 4,000 expert contributors, and its strict code of accuracy and objectivity, is ranked 5,128.*

But as I now know, it's not just Wikipedia that is deeply flawed. A great deal of Web content is not at all what it seems. What passes for "amateur" contribution is often, in fact, professional advertising, or political or other propaganda.

To take just one small example from Keen's book: On the fantastically popular video-clip-sharing site called YouTube, a short film was posted last August [2006]. It purported to be a rap video called *Tea Party*.

But it wasn't a simple home-shot-video like the ones that normally fill the site. It was, in fact, paid for by Smirnoff to advertise their new product Raw Tea, yet nowhere was this fact mentioned. The company instead hoped to market its product by stealth. Another YouTube success, lonelygirl15, purports to be a self-made videoblog detailing the life of an angst-ridden teenager. It is, in fact, cheaply but commercially made, with a twenty-something Australian actress called Jessica simply playing out a story that is every bit as fictional as any of the TV soaps.

The project turned out to be the brainchild of two Californian filmmakers, pioneering a new form of "viral broadcasting" which they hoped might generate sufficient hype to attract mainstream advertising. The ploy has worked. The video blog now attracts more than 11 million viewers, and makes money through advertising, product placement deals and donations from fans.

"So what?" you might say. "Does any of this really matter?" I believe it matters very much, because this was another example of falsehood masquerading as truth.

Undermining Ownership

I have only just scratched the surface of Keen's examples, but already we have an encyclopaedia which purveys falsehood easily outstripping one which is totally reliable. We have cunningly planted advertising masquerading as music videos, and true confessions turning out to be acting.

Magnified across the whole sprawl of the Internet, it is easy to see how truth itself has been made cheap by Web 2.0. And this is just the start of the problem.

If civilised life, and our shared perception of goodness, depends on keeping the division very sharp between truth and falsehood, then it also, surely, depends upon an idea of ownership. You don't pinch [steal] other people's property.

Yet teachers in schools, colleges and universities have noted a terrifying rise in what used to be called cheating—with vast screeds of students' course work often lifted wholesale from the Internet (though much of the material is often riddled with factual errors). This habit of mind—"If it's online, it's free"—extends to films and music, too.

The strongest point made here by Keen is that any film or music made by amateurs is very unlikely to be as good as that which has been put together by experts in a recording studio. Yet the Web is actually destroying the professionalism and talent of true stars by undermining the industry that supports them.

The habit of illegally downloading music onto iPods—which is piracy or theft when you do it to a commercially marketed piece of music—has not only led to the financial collapse of many record labels, it also imperils the whole creative process.

Just Another Version of the Truth

[Thomas Henry] Huxley's theory says that if you provide infinite monkeys with infinite typewriters, some monkey somewhere will eventually create a masterpiece—a play by Shakespeare, a Platonic dialogue, or an economic treatise by Adam Smith. . . .

Today's technology hooks all those monkeys up with all those typewriters. Except in our Web 2.0 world, the typewriters aren't quite typewriters, but rather networked personal computers, and the monkeys aren't quite monkeys, but rather Internet users. . . .

At the heart of this infinite monkey experiment in self-publishing is the Internet diary, the ubiquitous blog. Blogging has become such a mania that a new blog is being created every second of every minute of every hour of every day. We are blogging with monkey-like shamelessness about our private lives, our sex lives, our dream lives, our lack of lives, our second lives. At the time of writing, there are 53 million blogs on the Internet, and this number is doubling every six months. In the time it took you to read this paragraph, ten new blogs were launched. . . .

Blogs have become so dizzyingly infinite that they've undermined our sense of what is true and what is false, what is real and what is imaginary. These days, kids can't tell the difference between credible news by objective professional journalism and what they read on joeshmoe .blogspot.com. For these Generation Y utopians, every posting is just another person's version of the truth; every fiction is just another person's version of the facts.

Andrew Keen, Introduction, The Cult of the Amateur:
How Today's Internet Is Killing Our Culture,
New York: Doubleday/Currency, 2007.

The result? According to one veteran producer, Alan Parsons: "The glory days of selling epoch-making albums like *Abbey Road* or *Dark Side of the Moon* are over."

It's the same in the movie business, with Paramount, Walt Disney and Warner Bros all cutting the number of films made and creating huge redundancies in the industry, because their revenue from DVDs is plummeting.

Disney's sales went down by an astounding $1.5 billion to $962 million in two years, 2003 to 2005. The main reason? The evolution of Web 2.0 had destroyed their market by enabling films to be downloaded and shared illegally.

In other words, by pirating old movies and classic albums from illegal file-sharing Web sites, the young are guaranteeing there will be less and less money for new films and new music—in fact, they are causing the deaths of these industries.

Dangerous Addictions

Add to this the dark side of Web 2.0, which has enabled gambling and porn Web sites to expand exponentially, and you can see that what is taking place is not just regrettable, it is dangerous.

A recent study by Dr Nancy Petry, an expert on online gambling at the University of Connecticut Health Center, says 65 per cent of Internet gamblers are pathologically addicted, and that Internet gamblers are "far more likely to be addicted to gambling behaviour than those who frequent real-world casinos".

Why? Because you can play online poker all day, every day in your own home, as many students now do. "It fried my brain," confessed a kid from Florida who lost a quarter of a million dollars. Such sums, as Keen's book shows, are not unusual.

Keen also demolishes the idea—which I had held in my ignorance—that online porn was mainly for sad old men.

Among the examples he gives, the one that chilled me most was this 13-year-old, named Z, being interviewed on an on-line "sex magazine" called *Nerve*:

Interviewer: "Have you ever seen any pornography on the Internet?"

Z: "Obviously."

Interviewer: "How old were you when you first saw porn?"

Z: "I guess ten, but that was because they were, like advertisements, s*** like that."

Interviewer: "Do you know anyone who's really into Internet porn?"

Z: "Basically all my friends are."

Interviewer: "Are you?"

Z: "Yeah. I'm not like ashamed to say that. Most of the time my friends look at it, it's not like, 'Oh my God that's so hot.' It's like, 'Yeah, that's all right.' I like gothic porn."

As Keen says: "Thirteen-year-olds should be playing football or riding bikes, not sitting in locked bedrooms looking at hard-core pornography.

The Internet is transforming future generations into a nation of kids so inundated by and desensitised to hard-core smut that they've even developed favourite genres."

Every time you make a search on Google or Yahoo, they clock your area of interest. They are building up a profile of you.

The Loss of Privacy

So, the Internet has led to a fall in academic standards, the collapse of the music and movie industries; it has turned a whole generation into potential gambling and pornography addicts (with calamitous consequences). And that's before we even delve into the risks of private information such as health records or bank details being stolen online by hackers.

Less dramatic than this, but equally pernicious in my view, is the simple intrusiveness of the Internet. You think it is you using it. But Keen has made me realise it is always the other way around.

Every time you make a search on Google or Yahoo, they clock your area of interest. They are building up a profile of you. "You see," Keen writes, the more information they possess about us—our hobbies, our tastes and our desires—the more information they can sell to advertisers and marketers, allowing them to better personalise their products, pitches and approaches.

"But our information is not to advertisers alone. Everyone from hackers and cyberthieves to state and federal officials can potentially find out anything from the last movie ticket we bought to the prescription medications we're taking or the balance of our savings account."

This is an absolutely terrifying picture. What in hell—and I choose the words very carefully—have we all got ourselves into?

A purgatory is something from which you can get out. A hell is not. And although he advocates a judicious supervision of your child's Internet use and a sensible approach to the whole matter, Keen leaves me very uneasy indeed. Has not this revolution in fact pitchforked us all into a nightmare from which no escape is possible?

The Internet Will Fracture, Rather than Join, Cultures

Hervé Fischer

In this viewpoint, Hervé Fischer disputes the notion that the Internet will help our planet evolve into a utopian digital world in which everyone speaks the same language, English. He notes that already the Internet is becoming increasingly fragmented as more people around the world come online and bring with them their own languages and cultures. Therefore, instead of becoming more unified, Fischer contends, the Internet is evolving into a fractured network of individuals, in the same manner that the world itself evolved into a multitude of different peoples speaking thousands of different languages. As Internet users, Fischer advises that our goal should be to adapt to this culturally diverse communications network, not to homogenize it.

Fischer is a multimedia artist and philosopher. He is the author of the book The Decline of the Hollywood Empire *as well as of numerous articles.*

As you read, consider the following questions:

1. According to the Bible, how did the birth of ten thousand languages come about?

2. According to the author, why do individual cultures have "invincibility"?

Hervé Fischer, "The Internet Tower of Babel," *Digital Shock: Confronting the New Reality*, translated by Rhonda Mullins, Montreal, QC: McGill-Queen's University Press, 2006, pp. 74–81. Copyright © McGill-Queen's University Press, 2006. Reproduced by permission.

3. How, according to Fischer, will we have to deal with the multitude of different languages on the Internet?

The faithful of the Internet religion believe that digital globalization is the end result of human evolution. They invoke the prediction of [French philosopher Pierre] Teilhard de Chardin that at the end of the process of creation there will be a kingdom of the mind, of a superior human intelligence characterized by shared knowledge and wisdom. They see the Internet as the instrument of this evolution towards perfection and employ metaphors of a connective skin that grows to cover the world, or of neurons of a planetary hypercortex [an outer layer]. It's that old nostalgia, that time-worn myth of human unity that will return with the digital realm. [Eighteenth–nineteenth-century French writer] Chateaubriand, among others, had already spoken of the dream of a universal society: "The folly of the moment is to achieve a unity of peoples and to make a single man of the entire species."

Is the Web as unified as Internet devotees dream? Is it not in fact an ocean on which voyagers immediately lose their way? A complicated cacophony rather than a dream of unifying global connection? Perhaps we could say of the Internet what [Argentinean writer] Jorge Luis Borges said about old books:

> O Time thy pyramids. This much is known: For every rational line or forthright statement there are leagues of senseless cacophony, verbal nonsense, and incoherency. (I know of one semibarbarous zone who librarians repudiate the "vain and superstitious habit" of trying to find sense in books, equating such a quest with attempting to find meaning in dreams or in the chaotic lines of the palm of one's hand. . . . They will acknowledge that the inventors of writing imitated the twenty-five natural symbols, but contend that that adoption was fortuitous, coincidental, and that books in themselves have no meaning. That argument, as we shall see, is not entirely fallacious.)

A Metaphor for the Tower of Babel?

We could say that the same arrogance, the same will to power that the Bible tells us provoked God when men tried to build a tower that would rise up to meet him, are naively expressed today in the desire to create unified global communication through digital technology. According to the myth, we owe the birth of 10,000 different languages to God. In effect, to put an end to man's inordinate pride in aspiring to reach heaven by building this tower, God acted in a way that foreshadowed our current information society. He did not hurl lightning bolts or unleash other forces of nature to destroy this defiant tower; instead, he created the diversity of languages. Unable to communicate among themselves, the men could not coordinate their building project and deserted the work site. The abandoned tower fell into ruin. This myth involves the punishment of humankind, and we have traditionally interpreted it as being negative. But we should instead look at it as the birth of cultural and linguistic diversity, the will of God, and a heritage that is as precious and as necessary as biodiversity.

Aficionados of globalization also take delight in the fact that the Internet is promoting the spread of English as a universal language of communication. We are supposedly witnessing an American cyberunification of the world, progress for one and all. In reality, while the use of English is growing on the Web, it is losing steam. International Technology and Trade Associates, in its *State of the Internet 2000*, pointed out that of the estimated 308 million netizens [Internet users], only 51.3 per cent use English (less than half this percentage connect from North America). Of course, 78 per cent of Web pages were still in English, and 95 per cent of them were devoted to e-commerce. But, the report concluded, "as more users come online in Europe and Asia as well as the rest of the world, the Internet is becoming multicultural, multilingual, and multipolar."

By 2006, Internet development had confirmed this. The expanding array of languages on the Web has begun to reflect the importance of diverse linguistic groups.

According to UNESCO [United Nations Educational, Scientific and Cultural Organization] estimates, in 2000, English represented only 65 per cent of content, and this will soon drop below the 50 per cent mark due to the rapid rise of other languages on the Internet—mainly French, Mandarin [Chinese], Hindi, Spanish, Russian, Arabic, Bengali, and Portuguese. Specialists predict that in 2007, Mandarin will exceed the 50 per cent mark in terms of Internet content. The Web will soon become a Tower of Babel—in other words, multilingual.

In 2006, UNESCO stated that more than 90 per cent of languages have not yet appeared on the Internet, and about 3,000 languages will disappear if we do not work to ensure their survival. It is significant that UNESCO has proposed using the Internet to do the job (this, of course, poses a huge challenge for the poorest countries, many of whose languages are purely oral and have no alphabet).

The Web will soon become a Tower of Babel—in other words, multilingual.

A New Mental Structure?

A number of specialists maintain that the Internet promotes a new mental structure. Navigating via hypertext and the Internet's interactive links is, like the relationship of a glove and a hand, "an inverted reflection of our mental space, a sort of objective shareable mental space," wrote [sociology professor and writer] Derrick de Kerckhove, who emphasizes that "the true nature of language is externalized and shared thought." The idea is seductive, but it suggests an overly instrumented notion of thought. In attempting to objectify thought in our external relationships with the world and with other people, we are removing its autonomy from instrumented language, which provides its capacity to transcend social language and to oppose it. The idea of a connective, collective, or shared intelligence confuses the field with the ball that the individual mind throws at it. Even the Lacanian [after French psychoanalyst Jacques Marie Émile Lacan] concept of the importance of the Other—that is, of collective and interactive social language as structuring the unconscious—does not deny the fundamental uniqueness of the thought that participates in it. Grammar, syntax, and logic inform thought, and intelligence is based (etymologically) on the image of connections that we establish between things, but the unfathomable source of thought in each of us cannot be reduced to software or to hyperlinks any more than to grammar and syntax. If this were the case, we would think according to the architecture and logic of [Microsoft] Office, Windows 2000, or Microsoft [Internet] Explorer. Our logic stems more from our family and social structure.

We still spend more hours a day in the real world than we do in cyberspace.

In short, this objectified, exteriorizing, or "chosiste" [favoring things over people] notion of thought is too American, too factual. We cannot turn our mental spaces inside out like the fingers of a glove to objectify the structures of the Internet or the cyberworld. To do so would be to submit human thought to the structures of techniques and machines. Reduction to absurdity may help us here. [Greek philosopher] Socrates thought and communicated in the oral mode, not the written, print, digital, or multimedia modes. And I am participating intimately in Socrates' thought in spite of, and across, changes in technical modes of expression. Multimedia, fortunately, cannot change the thought of Socrates.

The Cyberworld Cannot Erase Culture

The cyberworld has taken root in our countries and in the streets of our cities. To say that the virtual space of the Internet is a sort of exteriorized objectification of our mental space is to forget that individuals, although they use the same browsers, have different cultural roots. It denies the overwhelming cultural diversity of our mental spaces.

Societal structures are as changeable as the cultures in which societies distinctively unite. And communication technologies have also changed a lot—from the archaic natural mode of the oral and the gestural to the most sophisticated digital multimedia; both forms coexist today, even in our most technologically developed societies. We still spend more hours a day in the real world than we do in cyberspace. And we must admit that the logical and rigid style of the German language corresponds to a culture, while the light style of the Italian language, with its aesthetic flourishes, corresponds to another culture. There are as many different images of the world as there are languages and cultures.

As the binary logic of computer language spreads worldwide, will it erase these differences and create a shared connective intelligence, standardizing mental spaces, imaginative realms, logic, and cultures? One could argue that thinking together does not mean thinking alike. But thinking according to the same grammar, the same syntax, and in the same words is the beginning of thinking alike. This is the level at which the identity of a culture starts to be forged.

Will the differences between Indian, African, Asian, and European cultures be dissolved into the North American form of thinking? Into Windows 2000? As an ordinary observer, and hardly a prophet, I would answer (as would the vast majority of us) "Never." Even brutal, intelligent, and enduring colonization has never been able to overcome the invincibility of a culture.

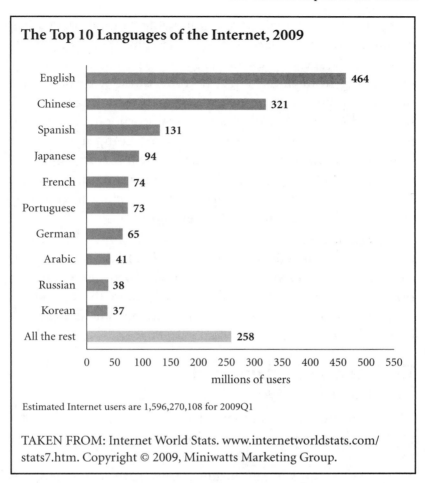

The Top 10 Languages of the Internet, 2009

Language	millions of users
English	464
Chinese	321
Spanish	131
Japanese	94
French	74
Portuguese	73
German	65
Arabic	41
Russian	38
Korean	37
All the rest	258

Estimated Internet users are 1,596,270,108 for 2009Q1

TAKEN FROM: Internet World Stats. www.internetworldstats.com/stats7.htm. Copyright © 2009, Miniwatts Marketing Group.

Cyberspace Will Be Forced to Reflect Human Diversity

Cyberspace is going to split apart like the continents, countries, and territories of the real world it reflects. It is therefore impossible to subscribe to the naive notion—which is far too widespread among digital technology zealots—that the Internet and the cyberworld will erase borders, territories, and differences by imposing the same objectified mental space on everyone. The objectified space of whose culture, whose language? American or Chinese? Yours or mine? There are many divergent mental spaces, immutable cultural origins that commingle in cyberspace without being absorbed by it; and it is possible to spend a few hours in an airport without the colour fading from one's skin. The cyberworld will split apart, diversify, and segment into a variety of cultural, linguistic, aesthetic, community, peripheral, marginal, corporate, and imaginative spaces—even if we use the same computer and the same browser to navigate it. Cyberspace will form within itself and increasingly reflect the human diversity found in the real world, because it is the creation and the technical, commercial, and cultural product of the real world.

Experience demonstrates that, at the individual level, virtual space has already split apart and is like a labyrinth. We each choose our own cyberworld with its own bookmarks in the course of our personal navigation. Amid the billions of pages accumulated on the Web, there are already as many cyberworlds as there are individual surfers.

The Internet of Cultural and Linguistic Diversity

We are seeing large commercial groups seize control of the media convergence of networks, software, and content, but the Internet is a web that in theory precludes domination by a central power, and it can encourage diversity in the end. Besides, democracy requires that these monopolies be limited and that a competitive balance among them be achieved.

The Internet is not simply a teleshopping centre for citizens who are reduced to the status of e-consumers. It also offers extraordinary potential for developing virtual communities, for the exercise of electronic democracy and the activities of opposing forces, as we saw in Seattle in 1999 [during the World Trade Organization protests]. The Internet is also the place for all self-media and for individual and local initiatives to be heard; it can give a voice to a group, an oppressed culture, a writer, or a marginal cause.

English will compete with thousands of other languages. The success of online translation systems will increase at the same rate as the diversity of languages that find new opportunities to express themselves on the Internet. While only a small minority of the world's population can connect to the Internet, we must also remember that for 90 per cent of this population English is not the mother tongue. The international organizations that predict that half the world's 6,000 extant languages will have disappeared within fifty years are extremely pessimistic—this is highly unlikely. We need to put the debate in a more realistic context. It doesn't matter whether television was invented by francophones or anglophones: Today it represents almost every language, as does radio.

Because the cyberworld emanates from the real world that it reflects, however powerful the unifying tendency of its technology and its founding symbolic system, it will not be able to slow the increasing fragmentation of languages used in it, its content, its community of users, and, consequently, its imagination and its values. Millions of people of different cultures who speak different languages circulate on our highways; while they travel the same routes in the same brands of car, they have unique projects and preoccupations. Likewise, a variety of people, also travelling for an array of reasons, meet and talk on planes without assimilating or becoming countrymen.

Globalization is both the naive dream of businesspeople and the exaggerated worry of pessimistic intellectuals. It is a superficial trend, one that will never take hold permanently. Besides, globalization is not all bad—for example, when it comes to the environment, human rights, natural disasters, and so on. And it is unreasonable to oppose the free circulation of ideas, people, and goods. However, cosmopolitanism is not a state that solidifies; it is unstable, vulnerable, and dynamic—whether it be in Hong Kong, New York, Montreal, or Paris. The world is not a computer, merchandise, a global market, or a Holiday Inn, and it never will be. If the globalization trend were to gain strength, then opposing forces would be unleashed. Peripheral conflicts are already arising, and so is a critical global consciousness denouncing environmental pollution, genetically modified organisms (GMOs), multilateral agreements, violence, excessive centralism, and the American desire to bring world trade to heel and reduce world cultures to the level of merchandise.

We must denounce this naive, damaging, and somewhat totalitarian technological utopia, this illusion that we can enter a better, unified cyberspace that would gradually replace the conflict-ridden, fragmented, and unhappy real world. Groupthink systems are dangerous. The fall of the Berlin Wall opened the door to an electronic capitalism that claims to be our savior and intends to rule the planet—an imperialism that is too sure of itself. As far as its enthusiasts are concerned, we will finally attain the goal of humanity through globalization, hyperliberalism, omnipresent digital technologies, triumphant e-commerce, and planetary communication that initiates dialogue and institutes individual liberties everywhere. We are witnessing an outburst of perverse neocolonialism, harbinger of false representations, dominated by magical thinking. Like any hegemony, it is already fated to collapse. Let's dream instead of the success of a multipolar world!

Online Translation in Real Time

The globalization of the Internet also creates a new need. If, out of respect for linguistic diversity, we refuse to adopt English as a universal language, we have to develop tools to understand the Chinese, Arabic, Finnish, and Japanese Web sites to which we will have access. A number of companies are working on this problem, offering online real-time translation systems that are constantly being improved and increasing the number of languages they can translate. These machine translation and text summary tools (Nstein, a Quebec company, claims to get at a text's DNA and unique meaning) combine dictionaries, linguistic research, intelligent agents (understanding tools), and a capacity for computer processing now available on servers.

The current demand for international communication and the many related markets will have us relying more and more on translation, whether for education, entertainment, or trade—we will need, for example, translated directions for the use of manufactured items. However, respect for cultural diversity and the desire for better translation will compel us to promote high-quality cultural adaptation—or localization— over word-for-word translation. Localization is indispensable, particularly for educational and cultural productions.

Online Social Media Offer the Freedom to Share Boring Content

J. Peder Zane

J. Peder Zane writes in this viewpoint that despite the communications breakthrough represented by social media such as Twitter and Facebook, the content of most "tweets" is mind-numbingly boring. Zane argues this has led to a well-deserved "Twitter backlash." Still, social media have given us a new freedom to communicate with others when we want to and have opened new doors in communications. Citizens can even follow the tweets of President Barack Obama and celebrities from around the world. Moreover, Zane claims, in our voyeuristic culture, many people actually seem to be interested in banal details about the rich and famous. The problem with Twitter and all social media, Zane contends, is not in the technology, but in our own limitations.

Zane has served as a columnist for North Carolina's News & Observer. *He is the editor of* The Top Ten: Writers Pick Their Favorite Books *and* Remarkable Reads: 34 Writers and Their Adventures in Reading.

As you read, consider the following questions:

1. According to Zane, what celebrities are making use of Twitter?

J. Peder Zane, "How We Love to Put Our Twitter Faces On," *The News and Observer*, March 15, 2009, p. Arts & Living D1. Copyright © 2009, The News & Observer Publishing Company. Reproduced by permission.

2. How much did Twitter use increase in 2008, according to the viewpoint?

3. According to Zane, what was human interaction limited to before social media such as the printing press, radio, and cell phones?

In our high-speed roadrunner world, you barely have time to lay an egg before someone tries to crack it.

So it goes with the instant messaging service Twitter.

The Twitter Backlash

Fifteen minutes ago it was the next new thing, the supercool cock of the high-tech walk. Now snarky Web sites, prestigious newspapers and even [Garry Trudeau's comic strip] *Doonesbury* are pecking away, depicting the 4 million to 6 million users it has attracted since 2006 as navel-gazing birdbrains. This flapdoodle already has a name: the Twitter backlash.

Splat!

Twitter may be twaddle. But it also represents a milestone in human communication.

Twitter is a free online service that allows people to send out short messages, called Tweets.

News organizations use it to send news bulletins to subscribers—car wreck on I-40, six dead in a plane crash.

Twitter may be a cutting-edge technology, but it is thriving because it taps into primal forces.

Celebrities such as Shaquille O'Neal and *Meet the Press* host David Gregory send regular Tweets to their peeps.

Not surprisingly, President [Barack] Obama reigns as the King of the Twits, with hundreds of thousands of people signed up to receive his blasts.

Concision is key. Tweets can have a maximum of 140 characters (20 seven-letter words). If brevity is the soul of wit, Twitterers must be a cross between [American humorists] Dorothy Parker and Mark Twain.

Only they aren't.

Boring Messages

Some Tweets may be pure poetry, but most are testimonies to the banality of humanity. Lunch plans, shopping lists and exercise regimes are popular topics. So, too, are close encounters with the boob tube: r u watching *Lost*?

The *New York Times* reports that a typical Tweet from Gregory informed his adoring public that, "It's 830. Rehearsal done. Guests should arrive anytime now. This is a good time for me to go thru my q's one last time. Maybe a bagel b4 air."

With butter or cream cheese? How about a schmear of grammar?

Twitter reminds me why I rarely check my Facebook page. There, dozens of "friends" I barely know provide steady updates that could be collected under the title "Being and nothingness." Their activities are so boring I want to cry—in part, because I'm doing pretty much the same.

It is easy and perhaps even necessary to bemoan the instant-messaging culture fueled by Twitter, Facebook and thumb-tapping cell phones. The recent series of *Doonesbury* strips lampooning the bland narcissism of Twitter were spot-on.

Nevertheless, we shouldn't blame the instant messenger.

Twitter may be a cutting-edge technology, but it is thriving because it taps into primal forces. The ranks of its users rose about 900 percent last year [2008] because it increases that most cherished human value—freedom, both for information and individuals.

Transforming Communication

Since cave people first began saying "ugh" and "huhn," human interaction has been limited. For millennia, almost all social intercourse had to occur face-to-face or through couriers and smoke signals.

The invention of the printing press and the development of the postal system dramatically increased the flow of information. The telegraph and telephone, radio and TV expanded it even more. More recently, cell phones and the Internet have empowered billions of people to reach out and touch friends and strangers in far-flung places.

Technology has transformed our capacity for communication, but its content is another story.

We are self-absorbed and we like to be in control. Twitter satisfies both impulses.

Banal, Eternal Questions

Prehistoric conversations around the communal fire were probably no more scintillating than the average Tweet. Life's deepest mysteries may always linger, but these are the eternal questions: How was your day? What are you up to?

Twitter allows us to do what we always have on a larger stage.

More troubling to some is the freedom it provides us to decide how we interact with each other. The Vatican sounded the alarm about this recently when it asked Catholics to give up text messaging for Lent. Its fear is well founded: People are increasingly choosing screen-to-screen over face-to-face communication.

Why? The answer, again, is human nature. We are self-absorbed and we like to be in control. Twitter satisfies both impulses.

The Sheer Boredom of Facebook

The reason to hate Facebook is because of the stultifying mind-numbing inanity of it all, the sheer boredom. If Facebook helps put together streakers with voyeurs, the streakers, for the most part, after shedding their trench coats, seem to be running around not with taut and tanned hardbodies, but in stained granny panties with dark socks. They have a reality-show star's unquenchable thirst for broadcasting all the details of their lives, no matter how unexceptional those details are. They do so in the steady, Chinese-water-torture drip of status updates. The very fact that they are on the air (or rather, on Facebook) has convinced them that every facet of their life must be inherently interesting enough to alert everyone to its importance.

These are all actual status updates (with name changes): "Maria is eating Girl Scout cookies. . . . Tom is glad it's the weekend. . . . Jacinda is longing for some sleep, pillow come to momma! . . . Dan is going to get something to eat. . . . Anne is taking Tyler to day care. . . . Amber loves to dip. I can dip almost any food in blue cheese, ranch dressing, honey mustard, sour cream, mayonnaise, ketchup. Well, I think you get the point." Yes. Uncle. Please make it stop. For the love of God, we get the point.

Matt Labash, "Down with Facebook!"
Weekly Standard, *vol. 14, no. 25, March 16, 2009.*

Direct interaction is unpredictable. One of the joys and tribulations of conversation is the pressure of real-time give and take.

Text messaging relieves that anxiety. We process the material on *our* schedule—say what we want, when we want. Or don't say anything at all.

Instead of forcing us to be our warts-and-all selves it allows us, at least in theory, to control the face we show the world.

Finally, it feeds our inherent narcissism, enabling us to prattle on without fear of watching boredom spread across another's face.

In fact, most people are not bored, because we are also voyeurs. David Gregory's report that he might eat a bagel is a crumb of intimacy that allows us to feel some connection to him. That we hunger for this precisely because we are choosing to spend so much time alone, in front of our screens, is an irony of modern life.

Twitter marks an advance in freedom. How we use it is up to us. The Twitter backlash may be necessary, but it is also doomed. For the fault lies not in our Tweets but in ourselves.

China Uses Harsh Rehabilitation Techniques on Young Internet Addicts

Ariana Eunjung Cha

Ariana Eunjung Cha reports in this viewpoint that the Chinese use harsh techniques to break teenagers and young adults free from what they believe is Internet addiction. Chinese authorities view Internet addiction as a serious mental disorder that affects a significant portion of the youth population. This belief is backed by some psychologists, according to Cha, including a handful in the United States. Skeptics, however, wonder if the Chinese authorities are using Internet addiction merely as a front for their larger goal of controlling their citizens. At a clinic in Daxing, Cha reports, patients are subjected to therapy that involves drugs, hypnosis, and even shock treatments. Whether these measures actually cure Internet addiction is arguable.

Cha is based out of Beijing where she reports on business and finance in Asia for the Washington Post. *She served as the* Washington Post's *San Francisco bureau chief in 2005 and covered the U.S.-led reconstruction efforts in Iraq from 2003 to 2004.*

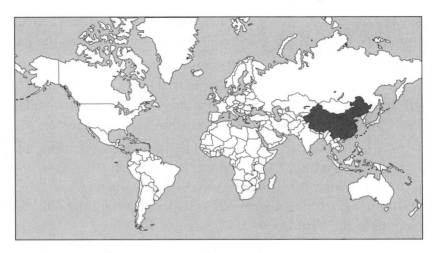

As you read, consider the following questions:

1. According to a survey, what percentage of Chinese teens are vulnerable to Internet addiction?

2. According to Cha, why is no one at the clinic comfortable talking about the third floor?

3. What does Sun want to do immediately upon getting home from the clinic, according to the viewpoint?

Sun Jiting spends his days locked behind metal bars in this military-run installation, put there by his parents. The 17-year-old high school student is not allowed to communicate with friends back home, and his only companions are psychologists, nurses and other patients. Each morning at 6:30, he is jolted awake by a soldier in fatigues shouting, "This is for your own good!"

Sun's offense: Internet addiction.

Fighting Addiction in China

Alarmed by a survey that found that nearly 14 percent of teens in China are vulnerable to becoming addicted to the Internet, the Chinese government has launched a nationwide campaign to stamp out what the Communist Youth League [of China] calls "a grave social problem" that threatens the nation.

Few countries have been as effective historically in fighting drug and alcohol addiction as China, which has been lauded for its successes, as well as criticized for harsh techniques.

Now the country is turning its attention to fighting another, supposed addiction—one that has been blamed in the state-run media for a murder over virtual property earned in an online game, for a string of suicides and for the failure of youths in their studies.

Few countries have been as effective historically in fighting drug and alcohol addiction as China, which has been . . . criticized for harsh techniques.

The Chinese government in recent months has joined South Korea, Thailand and Vietnam in taking measures to try to limit the time teens spend online. It has passed regulations banning youths from Internet cafes and has implemented control programs that kick teens off networked games after five hours.

There's a global controversy over whether heavy Internet use should be defined as a mental disorder, with some psychologists, including a handful in the United States, arguing that it should be. Backers of the notion say the addiction can be crippling, leading people to neglect work, school and social lives.

But no country has gone quite as far as China in embracing the theory and mounting a public crusade against Internet addiction. To skeptics, the campaign dovetails a bit too nicely with China's broader effort to control what its citizens can see on the Internet. The Communist government runs a massive program that limits Web access, censors sites and seeks to

Characterizing Internet Addiction Disorder

In some respects, addictive use of the Internet resembles other so-called "process" addictions, in which a person is addicted to an activity or behavior (including gambling, shopping, or certain sexual behaviors) rather than a substance (mood-altering drugs, tobacco, food, etc.). People who develop problems with their Internet use may start off using the Internet on a casual basis and then progress to using the technology in dysfunctional ways. Many people believe that spending large amounts of time on the Internet is a core feature of the disorder. The amount of time by itself, however, is not as important a factor as the ways in which the person's Internet use is interfering with their daily functioning. Use of the Internet may interfere with the person's social life, school work, or job-related tasks at work. In addition, cases have been reported of persons entering Internet chat rooms for people with serious illnesses or disorders, and pretending to be a patient with that disorder in order to get attention or sympathy. Treatment options often mirror those for other addictions.

Encyclopedia of Mental Disorders,
"Internet Addiction Disorder," 2009.

control online political dissent. Internet companies like Google have come under heavy criticism abroad for going along with China's demands.

In the Internet-addiction campaign, the government is helping to fund eight inpatient rehabilitation clinics across the country.

The Daxing Clinic Exists to Treat Addiction

The clinic in Daxing, a suburb of Beijing, the capital, is the oldest and largest, with 60 patients on a normal day and as many as 280 during peak periods. Few of the patients, who range in age from 12 to 24, are here willingly. Most have been forced to come by their parents, who are paying upward of $1,300 a month—about 10 times the average salary in China—for the treatment.

Led by Tao Ran, a military researcher who built his career by treating heroin addicts, the clinic uses a tough-love approach that includes counseling, military discipline, drugs, hypnosis and mild electric shocks.

If you let someone go online and then he can't go online, you may see a physical reaction, just like someone coming off drugs.

Tao said the clinic is based on the idea that there are many similarities between his current patients and those he had in the past.

In terms of withdrawal: "If you let someone go online and then he can't go online, you may see a physical reaction, just like someone coming off drugs." And in terms of resistance: "Today you go half an hour, and the next day you need 45 minutes. It's like starting with drinking one glass and then needing half a bottle to feel the same way."

Located on an army training base, the Internet-addiction clinic is distinct from the other buildings on campus because of the metal grates and padlocks on every door and the bars on every window.

On the first level are 10 locked treatment rooms geared toward treating teen patients suffering from disturbed sleep, lack of motivation, aggression, depression and other problems. Unlike the rest of the building, which is painted in blues and grays and kept cold to keep the teens alert, these rooms are sunny and warm.

Inside Room No. 8 are toys and other figurines that the teens can play with while psychologists watch. Room 10 contains rows of fake machine guns that the patients use for role-play scenarios that are supposed to bridge the virtual world with the real one.

Room No. 4 is made up to look like home, with rattan furniture and fake flowers, to provide a comfortable place for counselors to talk to the teens. The staff tries to blend into the artificial environment. Before meeting with a patient, one counselor swapped her olive military uniform for a motherly cardigan and plaid skirt.

The Clinic's Patients

Among the milder cases are those of Yu Bo, 21, from Inner Mongolia, and Li Yanjiang, 15, from Hebei province. Both said that they used to spend four to five hours a week online and their daily lives weren't affected but that their parents wanted them to cut their computer usage to zero so they could study. Yu said he agreed to come because he wanted to train himself. Li said it was because he just wanted to "get away from my parents."

Perceived as a more serious case is that of He Fang, 22, a college student from the western region of Xinjiang. The business administration major said his grades tanked when he started playing online games several hours a night. The clinic "has mainly helped me change the way I think," he said. "It's not about getting away from pressure but facing it and dealing with it."

Before Sun, the 17-year-old, who is from the city of Cangzhou, checked into the clinic about a month ago, he said, he was sometimes online playing games for 15 hours nonstop. "My life was not routine—day and night I was messed up," he said.

In December, he concluded that school just "wasn't interesting" and stopped attending. His parents were furious and complained that he didn't have a goal. Exasperated, they eventually checked him into the clinic.

Since he's been there, Sun said, he's decided to finish high school, attend college and then work at a private company, perhaps becoming an "authority figure" one day. With the help of a counselor, he's mapped out a life plan from now until he's 84.

Sun's father and mother, Sun Fengxiang and Xu Ying, both 41 and accountants, say their son's counselors have told them he's behaving well—playing basketball, reading books about success—but they are unsure whether he's really been cured.

"His language shows that he has changed, but we'll see" when Sun gets home, his father said.

The Third Floor Is for Serious Cases

No one is comfortable talking about the third floor of the clinic, where serious cases—usually two or three at a time—are housed. Most have been addicted to the Internet for five or more years, Tao said, are severely depressed and refuse counseling. One sliced his wrists but survived. These teens are under 24-hour supervision.

Tao said he believes 70 percent of the teens, after one to three months of treatment, will go home and lead normal lives, but he's less optimistic about the third-floor patients. "Their souls are gone to the online world," he said.

Earlier this month [February 2007], four teens fled their dorm rooms and jumped in a taxi. They made it to a train station before soldiers caught them, according to Li Jiali, a military guard. They were isolated and asked to write reports about why their actions were wrong.

Going Too Far?

Guo Tiejun, a school headmaster turned psychologist who runs an Internet-addiction research center in Shanghai, said the military-run clinic goes too far in treating Internet addicts like alcohol and drug addicts.

He said that he has treated several former patients of the Daxing clinic and that one mother told him it was simply "suffering for a month" that did not help her son. He advocates a softer approach. Guo said he believes that the root of the problem is loneliness and that the most effective treatment is to treat the teens "like friends."

"Our conclusion is that kids who get addicted in society have some kind of disability or weakness. They can't make friends, can't fulfill their desire of social communication, so they go online," Guo said.

Guo is especially critical of the use of medications—which include antidepressants, antipsychotics, and a variety of other pills and intravenous drips—for Internet addiction because, he said, that approach treats symptoms, not causes.

For all the high-tech treatments available to Sun [a patient] at the clinic, the one that he says helped him most was talking.

Defending the Treatments

Tao and his team of 15 doctors and nurses defended the treatment methods. He said that while some clinics depend wholly on medications—in one experiment conducted in Ningbo, a city south of Shanghai, suspected Internet addicts were given the same pills as drug addicts—only one out of five patients at the Daxing clinic receive prescription drugs. Tao did agree with Guo that Internet addiction is usually an expression of deeper psychological problems.

"We use these medicines to give them happiness," Tao said, "so they no longer need to go on the Internet to be happy."

Still, for all the high-tech treatments available to Sun at the clinic, the one that he says helped him most was talking. He looks forward to returning to school and getting on with his life.

The first task on his agenda when he gets home: get online. He needs to tell his worried Internet friends where he was these past few weeks.

In Bangladesh, the Internet Is Improving People's Lives

Kevin Sullivan

In the following viewpoint, Kevin Sullivan writes that the Internet is having a radical effect on the lives of people in Bangladesh. Medical information, weather reports, e-mail, and other Internet services are slowly becoming a reality for people who have no landline phones and often lack electricity and running water. Yet hundreds of Internet centers are opening around the country, reports Sullivan, enabling Bangladeshi people to communicate with friends and relatives all over the world. Entire families gather around computers to hold video conferences or even watch a couple exchange marital vows. In short, Sullivan asserts, Internet access is enabling one of the world's poorest nations to overcome poverty and isolation.

Sullivan and his wife, Mary Jordan, are Washington Post's *co-bureau chiefs in London. Sullivan joined the* Washington Post *in 1991. He and Jordan won the George Polk Award in Journalism in 1998 for coverage of the Asian financial crisis and the 2003 Pulitzer Prize for international reporting.*

As you read, consider the following questions:

1. As of the date of this article, how many cell phones do Bangladeshi people have, and how many others are getting cell phones each month?

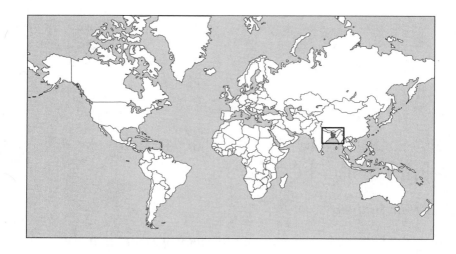

2. According to the viewpoint, what is the average annual income in Bangladesh?

3. According to Kevin Sullivan, what is one of the most popular services in the Charkhai, Bangladesh, Internet center?

The village doctor's diagnosis was dire: Marium needed immediate surgery to replace two heart valves.

The 28-year-old mother of three said she was confused and terrified. She could barely imagine open-heart surgery. She had no idea how her family of farm laborers could pay for an operation that would cost $4,000.

Essential Information via the Internet

The next day, September 16, her father went to see Mahbubul Ambia, who had recently installed the only Internet connection for 20 miles in far northeastern Bangladesh. Ambia sat down at a computer, connected to the Internet by a cable plugged into his cell phone, and searched for cardiac specialists in Dhaka, the capital, 140 miles away. He found one and made an appointment for Marium, who like many people here goes by just one name. The specialist examined her and said she needed only a routine surgical procedure that cost $500.

"I felt a very deep sense of relief," Marium said.

Villages in one of the world's poorest countries, long isolated by distance and deprivation, are getting their first Internet access, all connected over cell phones. And in the process, millions of people who have no landline telephones, and often lack electricity and running water, in recent months have gained access to services considered basic in richer countries: weather reports, e-mail, even a doctor's second opinion.

Cell phones have become a new bridge across the digital divide between the world's rich and poor, as innovators use the explosive growth of cell phone networks to connect people to the Internet.

Villages in one of the world's poorest countries, long isolated by distance and deprivation, are getting their first Internet access, all connected over cell phones.

Bangladesh Gets Connected

Bangladesh now [in November 2006] has about 16 million cell phone subscribers—and 2 million new users each month—compared with just 1 million landline phones to serve a population of nearly 150 million people.

Since February, Internet centers have opened in well over 100 Bangladeshi villages, and a total of 500 are scheduled to be open by the end of the year. All of them are in places where there are no landlines and the connections will be made exclusively over cell phone networks.

Before February, analysts said, only 370,000 Bangladeshis had access to the Internet. But now millions of villagers have access to information and services that had been available only by walking or taking long and expensive bus rides, or were beyond their reach altogether.

People now download job applications and music, see school exam results, check news and crop prices, make inexpensive Internet phone calls or use Web cameras to see relatives. Students from villages with few books now have access to online dictionaries and encyclopedias.

"We could not imagine where this technology has taken us in such a short time," said Mufizur Rahman, 48, a grocery shop owner in Charkhai, a town of about 40,000 people whose streets are filled with colorful three-wheeled bicycle rickshaws, and where there are almost no cars.

"For the first world, this is minor," he said. "But this is a big thing for us."

The Internet centers are being set up by Grameenphone, a cell phone provider partly owned by the Grameen Bank, which shared this year's Nobel Peace Prize with its founder, Muhammad Yunus.

The centers are building on a cell phone network created over the past decade by a Grameen Bank program that helped provide more than 250,000 cell phones in villages. When that program started in 1997, only 1.5 percent of the population had access to a telephone; that has risen to more than 10 percent.

Staying Connected

Goats grazed on litter outside Ambia's little Internet shop in Charkhai, where merchants sell bright red tomatoes and honking ducks in the crowded central market.

Bangladesh, where the United Nations says average annual income is about $440, is one of the most densely populated countries in the world, with its 150 million people crammed into an area roughly the size of Iowa.

Ambia's shop sits wedged between a stall where men sell huge sacks of rice and one selling cheap plastic shoes. By midmorning on a steamy September day, at least 20 people stood in line waiting to use one of Ambia's two Chinese-made computers.

A woman named Aleya, 55, sat down on a small plastic chair and handed Ambia a scrap of paper with a London phone number. She said that her 18-year-old daughter was getting married and that she was calling her uncle in England to ask him to help pay for it. Aleya said her husband is a construction worker who earns about $70 a month, barely enough to feed their five children.

Ambia dialed the number on the keyboard of his computer, connected by a cable to a Motorola cell phone. The call connected using VoIP (voice over Internet protocol) technology, which allows calls to be placed from a computer to another computer or a telephone anywhere in the world—for little or no cost.

VoIP technology is growing rapidly. One of the biggest brands, Skype, was founded in August 2003 and now has 136 million registered users. Companies such as Vonage and Yahoo also offer the service and are expanding exponentially.

"I used to have to make a plan and spend a whole day to make a call. Now I can just come in here [the Internet center] and relax."

Aleya picked up the small telephone handset connected to the computer and her face lit up. Her uncle, who owns a restaurant in London, promised that he'd make arrangements to send money for the wedding.

The five-minute call cost eight Bangladeshi taka, about 11 cents.

"An eight-taka call has earned me thousands," Aleya said with a broad smile.

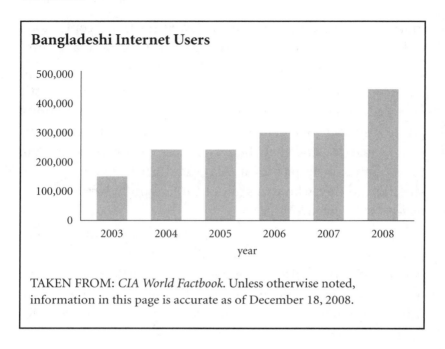

Bangladeshi Internet Users

TAKEN FROM: *CIA World Factbook.* Unless otherwise noted, information in this page is accurate as of December 18, 2008.

Before Ambia's center opened in February, Aleya said, she would have called her uncle on a borrowed cell phone at a cost of more than $2, her husband's daily wage.

The only other option would have been to take a bumpy bus to Sylhet, a city about 20 miles down the road, to make the call from an Internet cafe there. She said rutted roads and ancient buses making frequent stops often turned that into an all-day errand that would cost her nearly $3.

As Aleya spoke on the phone, Komoruddin, 50, was waiting to make a call to his son, an electrician living in Saudi Arabia. Komoruddin said he and his other son and five daughters live largely on the money his son sends home.

"I used to have to make a plan and spend a whole day to make a call. Now I can just come in here and relax," he said. "I never thought I'd see anything like this here. Some people still don't believe it."

Internet Centers Open Up Brand New Opportunities

Ambia, a lanky 26-year-old, said he was running a small shop doing cell phone repairs when he heard about Grameenphone's plan to create hundreds of village Internet centers.

"I love browsing the Internet, but I used to have to go to Sylhet to do it," he said. "When I saw the opportunity to combine browsing and business, I took it."

He said his business is growing fast, fueled by villagers' delight at being able to connect with a world beyond theirs. Ambia also sells cell phones in his shop, and each month he signs up about 500 new customers, who pay about $4 to activate a phone.

Ambia said Internet access is a logical next step in Charkhai's digital evolution. In recent months, he noted, local people have been making long walks through the fields and crossing wide rivers to log into cyberspace.

Before, getting a passport application could take weeks, or would require a bus trip to Sylhet. News of overseas job opportunities used to come by word of mouth. But now people browse online employment bulletin boards, then use the center's scanner to submit completed applications for jobs that before they might never have known about.

Students cram into the two-room center to use computers to check results of their standardized exams, instead of walking miles or taking a bus ride to get them.

Ambia has created a database of land and houses for sale around Charkhai, which better-off Bangladeshis in London or the Middle East use to browse for investments in their homeland.

He is working on databases listing doctors and other basic services. He said a program would soon begin to allow local doctors and their patients to hold video conferences to consult with specialists in Dhaka.

"People are just beginning to know about this," he said. "They are excited to get this kind of information."

One of Ambia's most popular services is video conferencing, using the little Hyundai Web camera mounted atop one of his computer monitors.

Entire families crowd in front of the center's camera to hold video conferences with relatives overseas. Ambia said a mother came in recently to hold up a newborn to give the father, working overseas, his first glimpse of his child.

"People even come here to see how things are being cooked in London, how they are cutting the fish," he said.

Weddings conducted over the telephone are common in this part of Bangladesh. Many marriages are still arranged between conservative Muslim families, and often the bride or groom is living overseas.

Web-Camera Weddings Create a New Tradition

And Ambia was preparing to add a 21st-century twist to a traditional ritual, by hosting his first video conference wedding.

Aslam Ahmed, 25, said he planned to sit in front of the Web camera in Charkhai and marry his girlfriend, Jasmine, 17, who would be in front of a Web camera in her home in London.

Weddings conducted over the telephone are common in this part of Bangladesh. Many marriages are still arranged between conservative Muslim families, and often the bride or groom is living overseas.

A marriage certificate is also a fast route to getting a work visa to leave Bangladesh—and conducting the wedding by phone is faster and cheaper than arranging for the overseas partner and family to travel home for a wedding.

An imam [Islamic mosque leader] is present at both ends of the call, along with a civil official who certifies the vows. Duplicate sets of paperwork are then exchanged by mail for everyone's signatures.

Ahmed and his bride had planned a wedding by cell phone and knew they would have to pay $30 or $40 just for the call. The video conference over the Internet, however, would cost a fraction of that, so the imams conducting the ceremony would not have to rush through the prayers to save money.

Jasmine's family moved to London in 1986. Ahmed said he had met her just once, in 2002, when her family came back to Charkhai to visit. They spoke on the phone and exchanged e-mail regularly after that—and once Ambia's center opened, they saw each other regularly by video conference, even though they live 5,000 miles apart.

"I don't know what other people say, but as far as I'm concerned she's Miss World," Ahmed said.

South Africans' Lives Have Been Changed by the Internet

Hadlee Simons

In the viewpoint that follows, Hadlee Simons explores the pros and cons of Internet culture in his home country of South Africa as well as worldwide. He discusses the wonders of the Internet, where every whim is indulged, as well as the dark side, where Web behavior has resulted in divorce and suicide. For all of its appeal and usefulness, the Internet may not be completely safe, Simons contends, and it may lead individuals to become increasingly isolated. However, whether or not one likes the changes the Internet has brought about doesn't matter. The fact is, Simons concludes, the Internet is here to stay, and South Africans should make the best of it.

Simons is a South African who writes for iafrica.com.

As you read, consider the following questions:

1. According to Simons, how is Diddit different from other social networking sites?

2. Why is the Megan Meier case a famous instance of the dark side of the Internet, according to Simons?

3. According to the viewpoint, what traditional activities have been replaced by Internet activities?

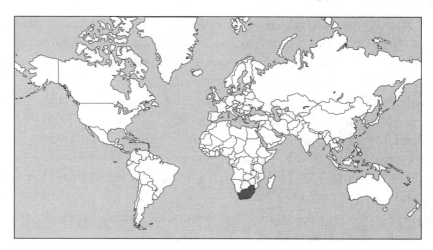

Remember the days of posting photos via airmail, waiting for your aunt in England to call for a few minutes and corresponding via letters?

The Wonders of the Internet

Thanks to the wonders of the Internet, finding your distant friends and family these days is a simple Facebook search or e-mail address away.

In much the same way that television revolutionised the way we receive information, the Internet has revolutionised the way we communicate, particularly in the area of social networking.

In much the same way that television revolutionised the way we receive information, the Internet has revolutionised the way we communicate, particularly in the area of social networking.

It has given us a new way to meet people, who we would never have ordinarily met—from the guys on the motoring forum who share your exact interests to The One on a dating site. The possibilities are endless . . . and weird.

Are you inflicted with the scourge known as herpes? Then www.h-date.com is for you—yes, a site dedicated to finding those with the same STD [sexually transmitted disease] as you. For people looking for something a little more middle-of-the-road www.freshmeet.co.za is the ideal place to start.

The wonders of social networking sites such as Facebook and MySpace mean that corresponding with your loved one (or not-so-loved-one) is a log-in away. Want to show your 21st [birthday] pictures to the world? A few clicks in Facebook and it's done.

Facebook also highlighted another interesting social dynamic: the status update.

Many of us have taken to writing and reading status updates. From the wannabe goth's depressing soliloquy, to the friend bragging about his latest conquest, status updates open new windows into the lives of friends and family. But sometimes Facebook and MySpace just don't cut it when you want to share something with the world. . . .

Diddit is another innovative social networking site that is rapidly gaining popularity. Ever wanted to brag about that bungee-jump experience? Diddit allows you to virtually tick it off—in other words, boast!

A Different Way to Connect

Another ingenious invention is voice over Internet protocol (VoIP). This allows one to make phone calls using the Internet for a fraction of the cost of a normal call, meaning that the days of expensive calls are numbered.

Web cams aren't new to the online scene but are no less a wonder. From your voyeuristic exploits to chatting with family and friends on www.stickam.com, Web cams give people the ability to enjoy an intimacy that voice chat can't provide.

Do you remember the days of playing video games with your buddy in the same room? The Internet has changed the way we have fun too. While not readily available in South Af-

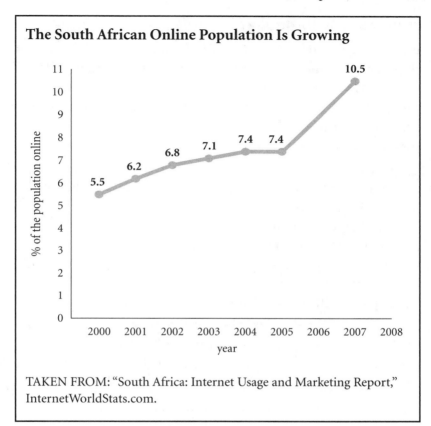

The South African Online Population Is Growing

% of the population online

11 — 10.5

0   2000   2001   2002   2003   2004   2005   2006   2007   2008

5.5   6.2   6.8   7.1   7.4   7.4

year

TAKEN FROM: "South Africa: Internet Usage and Marketing Report," InternetWorldStats.com.

rica, for the most part, playing online is one of the most refreshing experiences in the world. But be warned: You'll probably encounter a few morons along the way, such as one guy I met from Midwestern USA who asked whether South Africa even had Xbox 360s.

Taking online games to the next level, virtual worlds have become all-consuming, with *Second Life* and *World of Warcraft* becoming inextricably connected to real life. Well, sort of.

Second Life's virtual currency, the Linden dollar, is exchangeable for real-life money and one can use it to buy property within the game. But with the benefits of real life, come the vices—Briton David Pollard's affair on *Second Life* resulted in his wife, Amy Taylor, divorcing him in real life.

How Safe Is It, Really?

It's human nature to fear what we do not understand and new technology is one of those things. From soccer moms decrying the use of MXit [a South African instant messaging application] to politicians complaining about violent games, cyberspace is no exception. Many people fail to harness its true power as a communications tool.

You have to wonder whether their concerns are legitimate—does the Internet really have a negative influence on our youth? The case of 13-year-old Megan Meier seems to reinforce the notion that the Internet is a seedy place. A woman posing as a boy named Josh befriended the teenager and all seemed well. After six weeks, the tone of the messages changed. "Josh" sent harsh messages, such as "The world would be a better place without you." Megan Meier committed suicide.

Megan Meier was just the most publicised case; with reports of predators using the Internet to defraud and harm people, there are many risks to using it. For paedophiles, the Internet provides the perfect tool for deceit and exploitation.

Making a call and surfing the Net have definitely reduced the amount of time we physically see our friends and family.

However, it must be noted that the Internet has also seen a crackdown on paedophiles. Take for example the case of Canadian teacher Christopher Neil. The 33-year-old was caught after Interpol [international police] experts managed to reconstruct digitally "swirled" photographs of him molesting young boys.

Are We Becoming Increasingly Isolated?

So, has the Internet drawn us closer together or has it simply distanced us from the real world? Making a call and surfing the Net [Internet] have definitely reduced the amount of time we physically see our friends and family.

Web cams and social networking sites have given us the opportunity to communicate with our loved ones in distant places, but more often than not we are reduced to sitting on the outside, looking in.

The fact that we are so wired has resulted in us compulsively checking our phones and computers every few minutes, leaving people with no time to do the things that really matter.

We seem to be content to read and watch what other people are up to—our own real-life version of Big Brother [the dictator in George Orwell's *1984*]. From checking out your crush's blog, to watching what other people are up to, we unwittingly become cyberworld voyeurs.

Nowadays, people are probably more likely to leave a Facebook message than visit the person to deliver it. A rambling message meaning nothing can easily be sent to someone on the other side of the world. The fact that we are so wired has resulted in us compulsively checking our phones and computers every few minutes, leaving people with no time to do the things that really matter.

Activities like going out for a cup of coffee, visiting a friend's house or even hanging around at the local park have been forsaken for watching a pirated movie at home, playing *FIFA 09* [a video soccer game] or logging in to your instant messenger for hours on end. And to think that Phidippides [messenger in ancient Greece] ran 26 miles to deliver a message. . . .

In the end, whether the Internet has made the world a bigger or smaller place is irrelevant. This invention is here to stay, so make the most of it.

The Internet Will Undermine Serious Journalism in Australia

David McKnight and Penny O'Donnell

Journalists David McKnight and Penny O'Donnell observe that the business model for journalism is rapidly changing in Australia and that serious journalism is chiefly at risk. Despite the emergence of the Internet as a major news source, Internet news depends on the greater resources available to print journalists. Newspapers still do the majority of solid investigative reporting, and the Internet model does not encourage thorough investigations, the authors argue. Instead of in-depth articles, the Internet presents superficial and shallow soft news items that may be flashy, but often contain little substance. The authors conclude that the implications of this frivolous model are dire for the continuance of serious journalism, which at present, is financially and politically autonomous.

McKnight has served as a senior research fellow in the Journalism and Media Research Centre at the University of New South Wales in Australia. O'Donnell has served as senior lecturer in the media and communications department of the University of Sydney.

As you read, consider the following questions:

1. According to the viewpoint, what are three reasons why Internet journalism may not be as good as newspaper journalism?

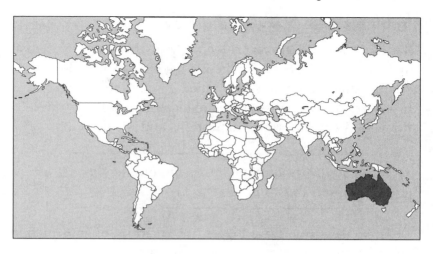

2. How, according to the authors, are online articles valued?

3. According to writer Nicholas Carr, what happens to the "bundle" of news and advertisements when journalism moves to the Internet?

Newspapers in Australia and the world face difficult choices in the next decade. The dilemma can be expressed in a simple question: Who will pay for quality journalism in the future? Until now, the answer has been obvious. Advertising has subsidised journalism since the mass market press emerged at the end of the 19th century.

But the much-despised advertising is on the move. It's heading for the Internet and with it is going one of the main props for journalists' salaries. In the language of economists, the business model for journalism is collapsing. But this is more than a problem for journalists or media owners; it is a problem for the democratic functioning of society.

Techno-optimists will tell you that the dinosaur newspaper industry simply will be replaced. The public will be informed by news on the Internet, television and radio.

Problems with New Media News

There are at least three problems with this bright forecast. First, newspapers are by far the main source of news as well as agenda setters compared with radio, TV and online, according to research for the Australian Broadcasting Authority in 2001 (now the Australian Communications and Media Authority).

In the language of economists, the business model for journalism is collapsing.

Their newsrooms are bigger, the quantity of information larger, the record of probing governments much more extensive and, with a couple of exceptions, newspapers conduct all the investigative journalism in Australia. The rest of the media feed off them.

Second, the optimists base their predictions on today's rich banquet of information and news available on Web sites. It's true we have never had so much information, including reliable news. Many people have given up buying newspapers and read them online.

But this situation is misleading. We are living in an interregnum [a period in between two monarchies] between the age of print and the age of the Net [Internet]. The content-rich newspaper Web sites in Australia and overseas are living off the assets of newspapers and their present advertising. Many non-newspaper sites, in turn, depend on them. If newspapers decline, the tap will be turned off and the apparent abundance of news will dry up.

Third, the optimists assume that advertising and news will jointly move online and the old cross-subsidy will continue. Wrong. Advertising online is much cheaper than print. Anyone can set up a classified car sales or jobs site, unlike a newspaper. The online competition is fierce. Online advertising will pay for fewer journalists' salaries.

The Progress of "Infotainment"

This will have momentous effects on the public's ability to get quality journalism, as opposed to recycled press releases.

The best response to this is one expressed by an editorial in the *Australian* in 2006 when the *Economist* magazine described newspapers as "an endangered species" whose survival lay in becoming more commercial. The *Economist* cited a profitable Norwegian newspaper that had set up an online slimming club for readers. It suggested this was a way of the future.

The editorial passionately rejected this: "The challenge facing newspapers is to respond properly to doomsday thinking by relying on their traditional strengths and reject research that tells editors the future lies in infotainment." Moreover, a commitment to quality journalism was good business sense. "Newspapers that allow themselves to be seduced away from the bedrock of good journalism do so at their peril," it said. "Content is king when it comes to media."

This is the route also taken by many British newspapers, notably the *Guardian*. It also involves an act of faith, since it is not clear whether the high road of investing in quality will pay off. But it is a refreshing and positive assertion in the "publish and be damned" tradition. The alternative is a more short-term perspective. This is symbolised by the practice of some online news sites. Here, stories are valued by their length (short is good) and by the number of hits.

A significant technique in selecting stories for publication and determining their phraseology is the use of "search engine optimisation". The latter inexorably drives stories towards celebrity and scream-in-the-night drama. To argue that the hits on online stories constitute a measure of its value is to blur market values with political and cultural values, to mistake quantity with quality, to confuse what is popular with what is good.

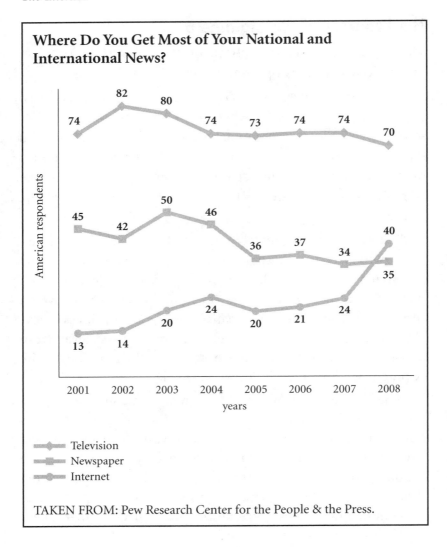

Where Do You Get Most of Your National and International News?

American respondents

82
80
74   74   73   74   74
                                    70

50
46
45   40
42   36   37   34
                                    35

24   24
20   20   21
13   14

2001   2002   2003   2004   2005   2006   2007   2008

years

◆ Television
■ Newspaper
● Internet

TAKEN FROM: Pew Research Center for the People & the Press.

But the problems of advertising and journalism run deeper than this.

The News-Advertising Alliance

British writer Nicholas Carr, in his book *The Big Switch*, uses the metaphor of bundling to describe the alliance of news and advertising.

The physical form of newspapers bundles together local, national and international news, analysis and commentary, photographs and TV guides along with classified and display advertising.

Advertisers pay to catch the reader's attention as they flip through this bundle. Says Carr: "When a newspaper moves online, the bundle falls apart. Readers don't flip through a mix of stories, advertisements and other bits of content, They go directly to a particular story that interests them, often ignoring everything else."

One of the journalistic consequences of unbundling is that "each story becomes a separate product standing naked in the marketplace. It lives or dies on its own economic merits." In other words, advertisements can be targeted to particular stories and advertisers pay the Web site only when a reader clicks on the ad.

In this way the tracking of click-throughs can be used as a measure of a story's worth. Carr predicts that "articles on serious and complex subjects, from politics to wars to international affairs, will fail to generate attractive ad revenues".

The decline of full-blooded political reporting, whatever its present faults, may have severe consequences.

The Severe Consequences of Unbundling

By contrast, articles on home renovation, personal finance or car performance can be expected to attract lucrative ad revenue, just as happens today in newspapers' lifestyle and products supplements.

The decline of full-blooded political reporting, whatever its present faults, may have severe consequences. Serious journalism—mainly from newspapers—not only provides a crucial linkage between politicians and citizens, but it also has the capacity and the power to intervene in political processes to scrutinise or avert potential abuses of political authority. In Australia, much of this is based on a simple constitutional and historical fact.

Governments can regulate electronic media through licensing. They do not regulate newspapers. If newspaper advertising and journalism are unbundled, newspapers will not only lose financial independence, but society will lose an important institution that has autonomy in the political field. Whatever newspaper critics may say, this move is likely to degrade the information available in a liberal democratic society.

Periodical Bibliography

The following articles have been selected to supplement the diverse views presented in this chapter.

Troy Dunning "Aging, Activities, and the Internet," *Activities, Adaptation & Aging*, May 2008.

Michael Gawenda "Papers Must Return to Core Business," *Australian*, October 7, 2008. www.theaustralian.news.com.au.

Nick Harding "Does the Internet Have the Answer to All Stupid Questions?" *New Zealand Herald*, May 11, 2009. www.nzherald.co.nz.

Steven Johnson "How Twitter Will Change the Way We Live," *Time*, June 05, 2009.

R. Kiley, G. Eysenbach, "Does the Internet Harm Health?" *BMJ: British and C. Kohler Medical Journal*, January 26, 2002.

Fengshu Liu "It Is Not Merely About Life on the Screen: Urban Chinese Youth and the Internet Cafe," *Journal of Youth Studies*, April 2009.

C. Frederick Risinger "Crossing Borders and Building Bridges Using the Internet," *Social Education*, November–December 2007.

Richard Stone "China Reins in Wilder Impulses in Treatment of 'Internet Addiction,'" *Science*, June 26, 2009.

Bill Wasik "Bright Lights, Big Internet," *New York Times*, July 29, 2009.

Peter M. Yellowlees "Problematic Internet Use or Internet Addic- and Shayna Marks tion?" *Computers in Human Behavior*, May 2007.

J. Zittrain "Saving the Internet," *Harvard Business Review*, June 2007.

GLOBALVIEWPOINTS

Chapter 2

The Political Impact of the Internet

In Canada, the Internet Is Slowly Changing Political Campaigns

James Mennie

Canadians have recognized the potential impact of the Internet on politics for at least a decade, James Mennie writes in the following viewpoint; however, the full impact of new media on Canadian political campaigns has been slow to evolve. No Canadian politicians have yet used the Internet as fully and successfully as Howard Dean or Barack Obama have in the United States, the author claims. Nevertheless, the Internet is becoming a force in Montreal politics, as the current mayor and his rivals have all established a wide Internet presence on a variety of social networking sites. The Internet has allowed candidates to reach a wider audience than before, Mennie claims, and has the potential to persuade more citizens to vote and become politically active.

Mennie writes for the Gazette, *Montreal's only English-language daily newspaper. He has served as a crime reporter and has written a regular column for the paper.*

As you read, consider the following questions:

1. According to Louise Harel, in the last Montreal municipal election what percentages of young people and all citizens voted?

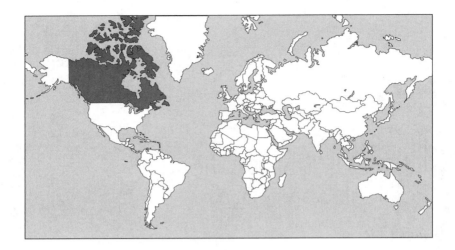

2. What Internet sites has Mayor Gérald Tremblay used to take his campaign virtual?

3. According to public relations director Mathieu Gagné, what old-fashioned campaigning strategy must politicians still use to gain votes?

It is still too early to fully know how important the Internet will become to the American political process. Right now, its relative importance may be low, but that will change, many experts say.

—Electoral Insight, *June 2000*

Four years after those words appeared on Elections Canada's Web site, Vermont governor Howard Dean turned conventional political thinking on its head when his campaign for the Democratic presidential nomination bypassed traditional media and fundraising channels and took the candidate's message to the Web and its social networking sites.

Four years after that, an Illinois senator named Barack Obama perfected the art of virtual, grassroots campaigning, and rode a wave of Internet-based popularity that took him to the White House.

This might be why Montreal mayoral candidate Louise Harel said late last month [August 2009] that the Internet did have a role to play in this city's municipal election campaign, noting that "it worked well for our American neighbours . . . it's one of the media preferred by the young generation, and I'd say that more and more older people are using it.

[Mayoral candidate] Harel's virtual portrait not only graces the Web site of Vision Montreal, but also directs visitors to her Facebook page, YouTube videos, Flickr pictures and Twitter musings.

"During the last municipal election, only 20 per cent of young people (those under 40) voted, while only 35 per cent of the total population (of eligible voters) voted.

"That's completely unacceptable."

Wired Politicians

And so, Harel's virtual portrait not only graces the Web site of Vision Montreal, but also directs visitors to her Facebook page, YouTube videos, Flickr pictures and Twitter musings.

Voters can see some of the social networking content without leaving the site, which was designed by Project Montréal. Users can also read candidates' blogs.

Harel's principal adversary, Mayor Gérald Tremblay, can be seen on his party's Union Montréal site. Until Friday, the site consisted of a slide show depicting portraits of the candidates running in the city's 19 boroughs and an archive of city statements, stock videos of policy announcements and tabs that would allow you to join the party or make a contribution to its war chest.

Now, however, Tremblay is as wired as Harel, YouTube videos and Flickr stills and Tweets bringing his campaign up to virtual speed.

"Click on Me! 2008," cartoon by Mike Keefe, *The Denver Post*, PoliticalCartoons
.com. Copyright © 2007 Keefe, *The Denver Post*, and PoliticalCartoons.com.

Tremblay says visitors to the site will be able to see a more genuine side of their mayor that's hitherto remained invisible.

"I'd like people to realize what they don't ever see. Not just the mayor at a press conference," he said this month.

"Something that is more private but still a part of public life. There are so many things that are happening . . . so I want someone to follow me and take all these pictures."

Hard Times for Hard Copy

There is also in Tremblay's strategy an admission that the medium of hard copy has fallen on hard times.

"People don't read," he said. "I have a 41-page document of what we've done for the past eight years. People won't read that."

But the mayor added that achievements in office can be accessed more easily—and visually—online.

"Look at (the renovation) of the Park/Pine Ave. interchange [in Montreal], a photo of what it was before and a photo of what it is today."

The three main parties in the municipal race are betting more on the Internet in this campaign than letting voters see and hear them 24/7.

Fighting for votes in a campaign where ethics will be a main issue, they've published a list of donations to their party on their Web sites.

Tremblay and Harel have agreed to call a truce in the traditional *guerre des poteaux*—the political poster campaign that seems to attach itself to every telephone pole and lamppost during an election campaign (although fliers, those irritating reminders of the democratic process, have been turning up on local windshields).

A Slowly Evolving Medium

The virtual battle lines thus drawn and the social networks marshaled, there remains but one question: Will any of it work?

"There has been no political party in Quebec that has managed to exploit the Internet as successfully (as Barack Obama)," said Mathieu Gagné, media and public relations director for Léger Marketing, a polling firm that surveys the ebb and flow of political fortune.

The Internet's immediate political effectiveness is that it allows candidates to directly address voters without their message having to go through the filter of mainstream media.

"And there's nothing to indicate that will change this time, either."

Gagné said the Internet's immediate political effectiveness is that it allows candidates to directly address voters without their message having to go through the filter of mainstream media.

He also suspects that getting those voters to log on to a party's site will, to a certain extent, be done the old-fashioned way, with campaign workers joining chat rooms to promote their candidate's cause and direct surfers to their party's site.

New Ways to Connect Politically

But in the end, Gagné perceives virtual campaigning—and any real votes they may garner—is a part of the evolution of political communications.

It was a process that began with whistle-stops and speeches delivered to voters by a single candidate, blossomed to an electronic, mass media campaign where radio and television narrowed political debate to a party leader's sound bite, and now can be found in flickering, one-on-one conversations on a computer screen.

"We won't ask politicians to go back to public meetings, if only because citizens don't have the time," he said.

"But anyone, at whatever time they like, be it in the middle of the night, and in a very personal way, can regain some personal contact with a politician online.

"With the Internet, there are no local or national issues, just issues that concern the voter. . . . And it isn't because the Internet is planetwide that it can't be used in a municipal campaign.

"If you can talk to the entire planet, you can certainly talk to all of Montreal."

Iran's Dissidents Use Social Networking to Challenge Government Power

Christian Christensen

Christian Christensen notes in the following viewpoint how social networking Web sites such as Twitter and Facebook have taken on a powerful role in the wake of Iran's 2009 presidential election. While Iranian officials have banned traditional journalistic accounts of the disputed vote and its aftermath, opponents of the regime quickly took to social media sites to provide Iranians and the outside world with continually updated accounts of the controversy. A battle over Internet control developed, Christensen reports, between the government, which used sophisticated technology to counter dissident reports, and the opposition itself, which continually tried to evade Iranian control. While the role of the Internet should not be overstated in the Iran controversy, the author argues, there is little doubt that social media pose a new challenge to authoritarian regimes.

Christensen is associate professor of media and communication studies at Karlstad University, Sweden; his work focuses on political, economic, and cultural aspects of global media.

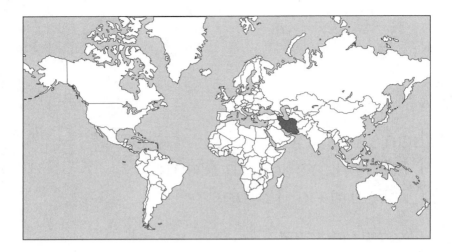

As you read, consider the following questions:

1. According to the viewpoint, how many Twitter followers did Persiankiwi and Mousavi1388 have?

2. After Persiankiwi's Twitter posts ended, what did followers speculate?

3. What is a "proxy server" and how did these servers affect communication following the election, according to Christensen?

On June 13, [2009], incumbent Mahmoud Ahmadinejad was declared winner of Iran's presidential election with a reported 64% of the national vote. His nearest rival, Mir-Hossein Mousavi, won—according to official figures—just under 34%. Mousavi and his followers immediately disputed the results; and widespread protests mushroomed throughout Iran of a size and nature not seen since the 1979 Iranian Revolution. As the protests grew in strength, the Iranian authorities cracked down on foreign media reporting in the country, disrupted cell phone use and text messaging, and restricted Internet access, making it hard to get information out of Iran.

Social Media's New Role

Enter Twitter and Facebook, which rapidly became vital tools to relay news and information on antigovernment protests to people inside and outside Iran. Although the authorities had banned access to Facebook during the run-up to the elections, users found ways around the restrictions and, during the demonstrations, Mousavi himself used Facebook to contact supporters and the outside world. As Ahmadinejad was calling the protesters "football hooligans," messages relayed via the social media (often repeated on global media outlets such as the BBC and CNN) showed the protests to be peaceful.

These events show the potential role of social media such as Facebook, Twitter, blogs and YouTube in facilitating protest and dissent during times of conflict and suppression—as well as enabling the spread of state propaganda and surveillance. The Iranian case reveals the new and complex role of social media in contemporary geopolitics. For traditional media such as newspapers, television and radio are often territorially bound, and thus subject to national laws (libel, censorship) and political-economic power structures (political pressure, ownership bias, advertiser demands); whereas social networking media are often decentralised, nonhierarchical and contain user-generated content.

> As [President] Ahmadinejad was calling the protesters 'football hooligans,' messages relayed via the social media ... showed the protests to be peaceful.

Two weeks after the Iranian elections, global "tweets" (messages posted via Twitter) on Iran and the elections continued to flow at an astonishing rate. A quick glance at twit terfall.com (showing which subjects are generating the greatest number of messages from Twitter users) towards the end of June indicated that tweets on Iran were coming in at over one per second, and showed no sign of slowing down. It took the death of Michael Jackson to knock the Iranian elections and the protests in Tehran from the top of the twitterfall.com list of most popular topics.

While the majority of tweets on Iran came from outside the country, a handful of highly influential individuals inside became vital sources of information, both for people inside Iran and for international news organisations whose operations inside of the country had been severely restricted (the BBC's Jonathan Lynn was expelled, the Tehran bureau of the Dubai-based satellite channel Al Arabiya closed, etc).

Two Major Protest Figures

Two of the major figures in postelection Iranian twittering were Persiankiwi (with over 39,000 followers) and Mousavi1388 (over 28,000 followers). Persiankiwi rapidly became one of the most trusted sources of information from inside Iran, with news outlets such as the *New York Times* and *Daily Telegraph* lauding her/his reports. On June 24, Persiankiwi's posts to Twitter abruptly ended, leading to speculation that she/he had been arrested.

Mousavi1388 (created by supporters of the candidate) also became an important player. In addition to the Twitter following, there was a Facebook page with over 5,000 friends, a YouTube channel with 31 video clips (watched a total of over 1 [million] times), and a Flickr photo-sharing page with hundreds of images from protests in Tehran. Combined, the two (with numerous other Twitter users based in Iran) posted thousands of tweets, with information on upcoming protest locations, government disinformation and propaganda, warnings of police and paramilitary activity, advice on medical care, links to news and information from outside Iran, still images and video footage of protests, calls to people outside Iran to offer their support.

Mousavi sent messages to followers via Facebook and by late June his page had over 100,000 "friends." Mousavi1388 even warned followers via Twitter that the Iranian authorities had set up two fake pro-Mousavi Web sites (www.mirhoseyn.ir and www.mirhoseyn.com) to trick protesters into disclosing personal information that could be used to locate and arrest them.

Iconic Images of Protest

Twitter, Facebook, YouTube, etc. also contributed to the dissemination of the iconic visual image of postelection Iran: video footage showing 26-year-old philosophy student Neda Agha-Soltan bleeding to death after reportedly being shot in the chest by a member of the Basij (the paramilitary voluntary militia). The video—uploaded to YouTube and published on Facebook by an Iranian asylum-seeker in the Netherlands whose friend had filmed the event on his mobile phone and mailed it to him only minutes after the killing—attracted well over a million YouTube views in under a week. Neda became the opposition's martyr figure.

> *The access to/posting of information . . . on social media within Iran has become one of the central issues in the battle between the Iranian authorities and anti-government protesters.*

The images of her lifeless eyes staring into the lens of the camera, blood flowing from her nose and mouth, have become as familiar as those of the young Kim Phuc running naked down a street during the Vietnam War, her skin burnt by napalm dropped from US military aircraft. Or the Tank Man who single-handedly defied a row of Chinese military vehicles in Tiananmen Square in 1989. Or Ahmad Batebi, the Iranian student who in 1999 was pictured holding up a blood-stained t-shirt that had belonged to a friend beaten by government authorities.

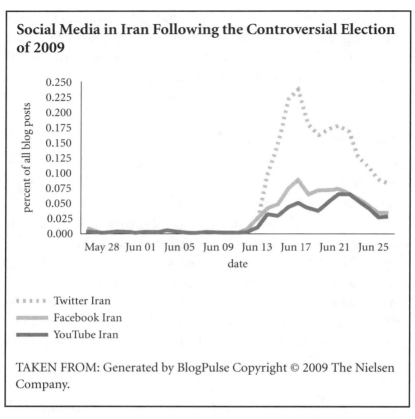

Social Media in Iran Following the Controversial Election of 2009

- ..... Twitter Iran
- ▬▬ Facebook Iran
- ▬▬ YouTube Iran

TAKEN FROM: Generated by BlogPulse Copyright © 2009 The Nielsen Company.

But what is different about Neda Agha-Soltan is that her image went out instantaneously across the world. Phuc, the Tank Man and Batebi had great impact but they weren't immediately incorporated into a freely accessible, digital and ever-expanding flow of information as Neda's was, to be archived, shared and re-shared by any and all with Internet access.

The Battle over the Internet

The access to/posting of information (such as the images of Neda and the tweets of Mousavi1388) on social media within Iran has become one of the central issues in the battle between the Iranian authorities and antigovernment protesters. The regime is engaged in a "proxy war" with Mousavi supporters: As access was restricted to sites such as YouTube, Facebook and Twitter, people in Iran began to use "proxy servers" to regain access. A proxy server is software that can be run on any computer; it allows an individual to "share" their computer (and thus their Internet access) with a stranger, regardless of location. A person in Iran, therefore, after configuring their own computer, would be able to use a proxy server to access unfiltered, uncensored versions of social media sites, as the "request" to access those sites goes through the proxy host instead of directly to the Web site (access to which has been blocked in most cases in Iran).

According to James Cowie of the Internet analysis company Renesys, these "open Web proxies" have become extremely valuable: "Iran's opposition movement has been vigorously trading lists of open proxies" via services such as Twitter. While some proxies were created specifically to help those inside of Iran gain access, many were created months or years ago and left dormant. Cowie's analysis showed that these open proxies were to be found in large numbers in the United States and western Europe, but were also being made available by users in China, India, Russia, Romania and Vietnam. In the case of Iran, the most obvious drawback of using social media to announce lists of open proxies was that as soon as the information was made available, Iranian censors would immediately identify and blacklist them. Cowie indicated that within two weeks of the elections, there were very few, if any, open proxies still available for use in Iran.

Christopher Rhoads and Loretta Chao disclosed in the *Wall Street Journal* that the sophisticated monitoring of Internet activity in Iran was made possible (at least in part) by technology provided to the Iranians through a joint venture between Siemens AG of Germany and the Finnish cell phone company Nokia. The Iranians, it was revealed, are capable of Internet surveillance on a much deeper and more sophisticated level than previously suspected. Using a technique known as "deep packet inspection" it is possible for the government, at a specific node known as a "choke point," to deconstruct and examine "e-mails and Internet phone calls to images and messages on social networking sites such as Facebook and Twitter." Rhoads and Chao said it was unclear whether or not the Nokia Siemens technology is being used specifically for deep packet inspection; a representative of the joint venture indicated that the technology was part of a larger contract to provide mobile phone networking technology. But what is clear is that the Iranians are filtering Internet traffic using extremely advanced technology, leading the country to be named by Reporters Without Borders as one of the "12 Enemies of the Internet."

Social media have made possible the presentation of alternative discourses to local and global audiences, challenging the orthodoxies of those in power.

A New Challenge to Power

Events in Iran should also make us aware of the dangers of sophisticated technology: The Iranian government used it to monitor Internet users and their messages; it served to simplify surveillance, disinformation and repression. With newspaper headlines such as "Tyranny's New Nightmare: Twitter," there's a tendency to assume that in the interrelationship between individual action, politics and technology, technology is the key. For instance, some mainstream newspapers labelled the antigovernment protests this April in the Moldovan capital Chisinau "the first Twitter revolution." Twitter was widely reported to have been the key in the efforts of journalist/activist Natalia Morari to organise the protests. Yet in the following months it was suggested that the role of Twitter had, in fact, been greatly exaggerated.

Though we should not over-romanticise technologies such as Twitter and Facebook, what we have witnessed in Iran was unique. The US State Department even asked Twitter to delay a planned upgrade to their system that would have disrupted daytime service to Iranians. Twitter complied, rescheduling the upgrade and ensuring the work would take place in the middle of the (Iranian) night. The State Department's request (which undoubtedly had more to do with US strategic interests than altruistic concerns for the Iranian protesters) shows its understanding of the potential of social media to recalibrate social and political power.

Politics has to do with the power to define what is right and wrong, what is legal and illegal, what is legitimate dissent or treason. Traditionally, it has used the mainstream media—newspapers, television, radio, film—to disseminate these discourses with production limited to a narrow elite, and with content subject to varying political and economic agendas. Social media have made possible the presentation of alternative discourses to local and global audiences, challenging the orthodoxies of those in power.

Technology Will Not Stop Evil Regimes

Abraham Cooper and Harold Brackman

Responding to a statement by Nobel laureate Jean-Marie Gustave Le Clézio, who claimed that Hitler might have had a more difficult time during the Internet age, Abraham Cooper and Harold Brackman argue in this viewpoint that no technological advance can stop those determined to perpetrate evil. Technological innovation, they suggest, has always been a double-edged sword. No sooner is technology put to good use than someone else figures out a way to counter that plan, the authors contend. China and Iran both provide present-day examples of how the Internet has been co-opted by governments playing Big Brother to their citizens. Technology alone cannot stop evil, the authors conclude, only people can.

Rabbi Cooper is associate dean of the Los Angeles-based Simon Wiesenthal Center. Brackman is a historian and a consultant to the center.

As you read, consider the following questions:

1. According to the viewpoint, what was the response of village elder Don Victoriano to learning from the Internet that Barack Obama had been elected president of the United States?
2. What is Red Flag Software, according to the authors?

3. According to the viewpoint, how many hate Web sites were operating on the Internet as of 2009?

"Who knows," Jean-Marie Gustave Le Clézio told the Swedish Academy when he picked up his 2008 Nobel Prize for literature, "if the Internet had existed at the time, perhaps Hitler's criminal plot would not have succeeded—ridicule might have prevented it from ever seeing the light of day." So do the dramatic protests in Iran, dubbed the Twitter revolution by some, make the French writer a prophet in his own time?

Cyberfreedom's Limitless Promise

There's no doubt that cyberfreedom's promise is limitless, its palpable impact truly global. Evidence: Blogger Xeni Jardin, who visited a remote Guatemalan village without television or telephone landlines but with a few cell phones and a nearby Internet café. Village elder Don Victoriano absorbed the news of Barack Obama's presidential victory over his Hotmail account: "If a black man can enter the Casa Blanca [White House], maybe a Mayan person one day can become president of Guatemala."

In the 1960s, [Canadian scholar] Marshall McLuhan trumpeted the emerging "global village" in which "the medium is the message." Today, it still is for those who see the Internet as the herald of a new interactive politics of citizen activism via social networking, e-mail petitions, virtual town meetings and online organizing. Those who viewed Mr. Obama's campaign as the coming of age of "the Net generation" also point to other global manifestations—from Ukraine's cell phone-driven Orange Revolution [2004 protests] to South Korea's "mad cow" protests against tainted meat imports orchestrated by text messaging teenagers.

In terms of historical hypotheticals, it's possible to imagine digital technologies—from Web sites to cell phones and text messaging—making a real difference. Just think if these options were available to Soviet dissidents and refuseniks who, back in the 1970s, were limited to communicating by handwritten *samizdat* [dissident activity]. Maybe *glasnost* [openness] and *perestroika* [reforms] would have come a decade earlier. Or just possibly there would have been a different outcome in Tiananmen Square in 1989 had Chinese protesters been able to communicate—and organize—instantaneously.

Internet Freedom Is Overstated

Or maybe not. It remains to be seen whether real tanks or thuggish shock troops such as Iranian President Mahmoud Ahmadinejad's Basij militia can be ultimately trumped by virtual protests. Would YouTube posts from inside the Munich beer hall where Hitler launched his abortive 1923 putsch [overthrow of a government] have made the Nazis look ridiculous—or, more likely, created a cult following among young people in search of a strong leader? Would smuggled cell phone videos from Auschwitz [Nazi concentration camp] have horrified and mobilized the German public or world public opinion to stop the factory of death? Not likely, given that the images of mass murder actually sent back home by Germany's "willing executioners" failed to change anything.

There's little reason to believe the Internet could have stopped genocide in 20th-century Europe any more than it has in 21st-century Africa.

In 2009, regimes such as Myanmar [formerly Burma] nip the problem of potential protest on the Internet in the bud by outlawing the Web: no medium, no message. But others, from China to Iran, take a more sophisticated approach. The Chinese government, with the complicity of gatekeepers such as Google and Yahoo, has found ways to squelch Internet dissent even while economically exploiting the Web. Beijing is forcing Internet cafés to switch to state-controlled Red Flag Software, ostensibly because "it makes sense for Internet cafés to use

[Red Flag] because of their high user traffic and the system's safeguards against viruses." The "viruses" that can be screened out extend to the [American rock band] Guns N' Roses album *Chinese Democracy*.

There's little reason to believe the Internet could have stopped genocide in 20th-century Europe any more than it has in 21st-century Africa.

Tehran seems to be going further. Finnish-German telecom equipment maker Nokia Siemens has been criticized for selling eavesdropping technology to Iran that Iranian authorities allegedly used to track online dissent during the recent postelection protests. And they are using Internet technologies to confuse tweeters with disinformation, a campaign that even extends to denying the martyrdom of Neda [Agha-Soltan, shot by a militiaman during a protest], the symbol of Iranians' civil outcry.

As Big Brother [oppressive] regimes manipulate the Internet, extremist movements strive to exploit it. In 1995, when the Simon Wiesenthal Center began tracking online hate, there was one hate Web site. Today [in 2009], there are more than 10,000.

A Double-Edged Sword

Let's face it: From the invention of the printing press to the telegraph, to radio and television and to the Internet, innovation has always been a double-edged sword. Contrary to the technological utopians, there is no such thing as an invention whose potential for good cannot be perverted for evil.

The upbeat age of Obama, unfortunately, is also an ominous era of Internet hatred. Marshall McLuhan's "global village" has indeed arrived—but it's populated by the good, bad and ugly of humanity. Mr. Le Clézio, the Nobel laureate, should stop hyping technological bells and whistles and stick

YOUR REIGN OF TERROR IS OVER EVIL DRAGON, FOR I HAVE
SLAIN YOUR INTERNET SERVICE PROVIDER!

"Your reign of terror is over evil dragon, for I have slain your internet service provider!" cartoon by Ralph Hagen. Copyright © Ralph Hagen. Reproduction rights available from CartoonStock.com.

to writing books that appeal to our better angels. Technology will never deliver us from evil. Only decent people can.

> *Contrary to the technological utopians, there is no such thing as an invention whose potential for good cannot be perverted for evil.*

Let's all commit to helping Tehran's tweeters survive the high-tech inquisition that's being implemented by reactionary mullahs [religiously educated men] armed with cutting-edge tools Hitler never dreamed of.

The Internet Will Save China

Liu Xiaobo

Jailed dissident Liu Xiaobo, a writer and prominent figure in the 1989 student uprising in China, maintains in the following viewpoint that the Internet is a gift from God to aid the cause of Chinese democracy. Upon his release from jail, Xiaobo was skeptical about using computers, but he was soon won over by the ease and efficacy of digital communication. Protest letters have always been a key strategy for opposing dictatorships, and the digital revolution has facilitated the writing and dissemination of such dissent. Not only can the Internet create entertainment stars, Xiaobo writes; it can also create truth-telling stars.

Xiaobo was awarded the 2009 PEN/Barbara Goldsmith Freedom to Write Award. He is a prominent dissident writer who has been held under house arrest in Beijing, China.

As you read, consider the following questions:

1. According to Xiaobo, what was his first attempt at writing on the computer like?
2. According to the viewpoint, what dissident letters preceded the 1989 Chinese student rebellion?
3. According to the author, for what did Chinese officials have to apologize as a result of news on the Internet?

Today there are more than 100 million Internet users in China. The Chinese government is ambivalent towards it.

Liu Xiaobo, "The Internet Is God's Present to China," *The Times* (UK), April 28, 2009.

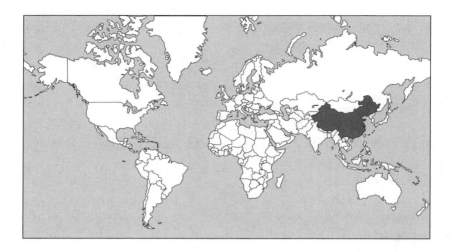

On the one hand, the Internet is a tool to make money. On the other, the Communist dictatorship is afraid of freedom of expression.

The Internet has brought about the awakening of ideas among the Chinese. This worries the government, which has placed great importance on blocking the Internet to exert ideological control.

The Magic of the Internet

In October 1999 I finished three years of jail and returned home. There was a computer there and it seemed that every visiting friend was telling me to use it. I tried a few times, but felt that I could not write anything while facing a machine and insisted on writing with a fountain pen. Slowly, under the patient persuasion and guidance of my friends, I got familiar with it and cannot leave it now. As someone who writes for a living, and as someone who participated in the 1989 democracy movement, my gratitude towards the Internet cannot be easily expressed.

My first essay on the computer took a week to do—I was ready to abandon it several times. Under the encouragement of my friends, I finished it. For the first time, I sent an article by e-mail. Several hours later, I received the reply from the editor. This made me aware of the magic of the Internet.

With the censorship here [in China], my essays can only be published overseas. Before using the computer, my handwritten essays were difficult to correct and the cost of sending them was high. To avoid the articles being intercepted, I often went from the west side of the city to the east side where I had a foreign friend who owned a fax machine.

The Internet has made it easier to obtain information, contact the outside world and submit articles to overseas media. It is like a superengine that makes my writing spring out of a well. The Internet is an information channel that the Chinese dictators cannot fully censor, allowing people to speak and communicate, and it offers a platform for spontaneous organisation.

The Internet has made it easier to obtain information, contact the outside world and submit articles to overseas media. It is like a superengine that makes my writing spring out of a well.

Before the Internet

Open letters signed by individuals or groups are an important way for civilians to resist dictatorship and fight for freedom. The open letter from [Czech writer and politician] Václav Havel to the Czech dictator [Gustáv] Husák was a classic of civil opposition to dictatorship.

Fang Lizhi, a famous dissident, wrote an open letter to Deng Xiaoping, China's leader, to ask for the release of the political prisoner Wei Jingsheng. This was followed by two open letters, signed by 33 and 45 people. These three open letters were regarded as the prelude to the 1989 democracy movement, when open letters rose up like bamboo shoots after rain to support the protesting students.

Back then it took a lot of time and resources to organise an open letter. Preparations began a month before; organisers had to be found to look up the people. We talked about the content of the letter, the phrasing, the timing, and it took several days to reach consensus. Afterwards, we had to find a place to typeset the handwritten open letter and then make several copies. After proofing the document, the most time-consuming thing was to collect the signatures. Since the government was monitoring the telephones of sensitive people, we had to ride our bicycles in all directions of Beijing.

In an era without the Internet, it was impossible to collect the signatures of several hundred people, and it was also impossible to disseminate the news rapidly all over the world. At the time, the influence of and the participation in letter-writing campaigns were all quite limited. We worked for many days, and in the end, we would only get a few dozen people to sign. The letter-signing movements in this new era have made a quantum leap.

The ease, openness and freedom of the Internet have caused public opinion to become very lively in recent years.

Beyond Government Control

The government can control the press and television, but it cannot control the Internet. The scandals that are censored in the traditional media are disseminated through the Internet. The government now has to release information and officials may have to publicly apologise.

The first senior official to apologise was in 2001 when Zhu Rongji, who was then the premier, apologised for an explosion in a school that caused the death of 41 people. At the same time, under the impact of Internet opinion, the authorities had to punish officials—for SARS [a respiratory illness], mining accidents and the contamination of the Songhua River [in northeast China].

Internet Activism Brings Real Results

Under the [Chinese] state censorship system, online discussions are most limited to politically acceptable topics. . . . However within these boundaries, Internet-enabled activism . . . has not only expanded traditional media reporting, but has also contributed to political results on those issues. On March 17, 2003, Sun Zhigang, a twenty-seven-year-old college graduate . . . was stopped by police. He was detained for not having proper identity papers and died in custody three days later. After the authorities refused to investigate the circumstances of his death, Sun's parents posted background information on his case and a petition letter on the Internet. His case was picked up by a reporter from the *Southern Metropolis News* . . . and then the story hit the Net [Internet]. . . .

Almost immediately, the case was being discussed throughout Chinese cyberspace. . . . Police brutality is not new in China. International human rights organizations . . . have called for abolishment of the custody and repatriation system, an administrative procedure established in 1982 by which the police can detain nonresidents if they do not have a temporary resident permit and return them to their place of origin. It was this inherently arbitrary form of administrative detention under which Sun was held. But the explosive reaction from Internet users to Sun's case was unprecedented. The official media, including China Central Television, soon picked up on the public outrage and reported heated debates over treatment of migrants living in the cities and police corruption.

On May 29, in an unprecedented appeal to the National People's Congress, four professors . . . called on the state prosecutor to investigate Sun's death. Three months later, the government abolished the entire custody and repatriation system, and the officials responsible for Sun Zhigang's death were convicted in court.

Lionel M. Jensen and Timothy B. Weston, eds.,
China's Transformations: The Stories Beyond the Headlines,
Lanham, MD: Rowman & Littlefield, 2007.

The Internet has the extraordinary ability to create stars. Not only can it produce entertainment stars, it can also create "truth-speaking heroes". It has allowed a new generation of intellectuals to emerge and created folk heroes such as the military doctor Jiang Yanyong (who publicly warned about the threat of SARS and forced the government to take action).

The government can control the press and television, but it cannot control the Internet. The scandals that are censored in the traditional media are disseminated through the Internet.

Chinese Christians say that although the Chinese lack any sense of religion, their God will not forsake the suffering Chinese people. The Internet is God's present to China. It is the best tool for the Chinese people in their project to cast off slavery and strive for freedom.

In England, the Internet Has the Potential to Engage Voters in the Political System

Peter Kellner

According to Peter Kellner, representative democracy in Britain, which has previously depended on access to privileged information by members of Parliament, must evolve now that ordinary citizens can access information from the Internet and become "expert citizens." He explains, in the following viewpoint, how the numerous advantages of the Internet's opening up of information and giving a political voice to ordinary citizens are tempered by the difficulty of ensuring quality control of the available information. Kellner predicts a massive cultural change in which ordinary citizens engage in politics. He envisions both a negative scenario that will destroy representative democracy, and more optimistically, a positive outcome where ordinary citizens adapt to the universality of available information and become increasingly involved in political decisions.

Kellner is a journalist, political commentator, and president of the YouGov opinion polling organization in the United Kingdom.

As you read, consider the following questions:

1. What does Kellner mean by "disintermediation" in the world of information?

Peter Kellner, "Expert Citizens," *New Statesman*, October 20, 2008, pp. 4–7. Copyright © 2008 New Statesman, Ltd. Reproduced by permission.-

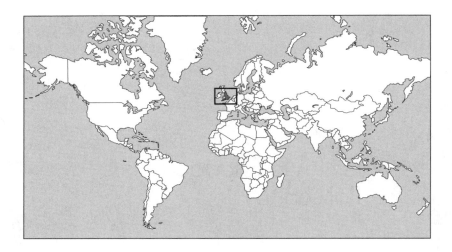

2. According to Kellner, what are some of the disadvantages of the Internet information explosion?

3. What does Kellner mean by the scenario of "reinvention"?

Whether you trace its origins to ancient Athens, or to Rome, or to England in the Middle Ages, representative democracy has had a long run. Is it now about to come to an end, swept aside by the Internet? Or will it emerge triumphant: challenged, changed and perhaps improved by modern information technology, but not destroyed?

My short answer is: It will probably have to cede ground to direct democracy, but unless we collectively screw things up on a massive scale—which is certainly possible—representative democracy will probably survive.

Why Representative Democracy Works

Here is my longer answer. Representative democracy is rooted in two distinct propositions. One has been the subject of debates about political philosophy for many years. The other has been largely unspoken but arguably provides the more important explanation of its survival.

The overt argument—set out, for example, by [British statesman and political philosopher] Edmund Burke more than 200 years ago—is that our representatives are able to reflect our values and look after our interests better if they exercise their own judgment on the great issues of the day, rather than simply act as our mandated delegates. They have more time to explore difficult issues, are able to consider the consequences of alternative policies, can consider trade-offs between conflicting objectives, and are less likely than mass gatherings to be swayed by irrational emotions. They have a vested interest in getting things right; for if they pursue policies that, however popular [they] are at the time, prove disastrous, they can be thrown out at the next election. Representative democracy offers accountability. Who can the public blame if policies they themselves approve at mass meetings or in referendums go badly wrong?

These remain compelling arguments. But there is something else that has made representative democracy the dominant form of government in so much of the world. This is the bit that the textbooks tend to ignore. As an economist would put it, representative democracy has enjoyed a technical monopoly. That is, as government has become more complex, it has generated ever-greater amounts of information and analysis on which to base its decisions. Whatever the philosophical case for representative democracy, there was a compelling practical case: Only a relatively small number of people, gathering in one place, could conceivably receive and study the documents that needed to be studied to reach sensible decisions.

I'm not saying every MP [member of Parliament] studies every government document: that would plainly be daft. But they have traditionally had free access to far more information, far faster, than normal citizens. To take just one example: At the end of every Budget speech, MPs can go to the Vote Office and collect the "Red Book" and all the other documents that set out the Chancellor's case in detail. Until recently, the rest of us would have to wait until the "Red Book" arrived at our local bookshop. And then we would have to shell out a fair sum for it. (A hard copy of this year's "Red Book" costs £45.) The key word is access. MPs had it; most of the rest of us didn't. That made representative democracy largely impregnable.

The Internet Makes Information Accessible

The Internet has changed all that. The "Red Book" is available to anyone, wherever in the world, at precisely the same time as MPs—and for free. There is no reason why that should not apply to any information or analysis that any government minister provides to Parliament. Suddenly, access to the playing field between MPs and citizens has been levelled. Representative democracy has lost its technical monopoly.

To make a stab at the likely consequences of this new world of instant, total information, we need to cast our eyes over another related trend—disintermediation. Originally this was used to describe the process whereby people took their money out of banks and collective savings vehicles such as unit trusts and invested it in particular shares or bonds. They were switching from mediated to direct investments.

Today the information process looks less like a rigid pipeline and more like a plate of spaghetti. It flows in all sorts of directions and in a large number of ways.

Now the word is being used to describe the way more of us are informing ourselves about the world about us. We used to rely almost totally on the media. The very word "media" described what happened. Journalists gathered raw information and decided what we should be told, and how. It was a classic mediated process. It operated like a pipeline with a filter in the middle. Information entered at one end, was intercepted by the media, and the filtered stories finally reached us. Our political culture reflected, and still largely reflects, this system—it's top-down, and we are largely passive recipients (except at election time) of what "they" choose to tell us and decide for us.

Advantages and Dangers

Today the information process looks less like a rigid pipeline and more like a plate of spaghetti. It flows in all sorts of directions and in a large number of ways. We can discover what we need to know without reading, watching or listening to a single conventional journalist (or, for that matter, politician).

This has benefits and drawbacks for the culture of democracy. The benefits include access to a far wider array of information than we had when we relied on the papers and broadcasters. Going online, we can now access stupendous amounts of information from national and local government. We can read debates in Parliament verbatim. We can access all the commentary and analysis we could want on any topic, from climate change to immigration. We can add our own voice, so we are no longer passive recipients of what the media chooses to tell us; we can act as angry voters or citizen-journalists to set out our views and news.

As a pollster, I see some of the uncomfortable advantages of this. Uncomfortable because there are expert bloggers out there—such as Mike Smithson of Politicalbetting.com—who provide challenging expert commentary on YouGov and other polling companies. Constant expert commentary keeps us on our toes. Four years ago YouGov joined with the other main polling organisations to set up the British Polling Council, whose main objective is to promote transparency. All members are obliged to provide full information on our Web sites about our published media polls. I suspect that without the Internet, we would not have acted to offer such transparency.

That is just one example from my own world, but we are not alone. The information explosion has exposed anyone who supplies it to levels of critical, public scrutiny that far outstrip anything the media used to provide, except on whatever topic happened temporarily to obsess them at any given moment.

If there are clear advantages, there are also clear dangers. Quality control is the greatest. We can't be sure that what we read on the Internet is true. (Note, for example, the way Wikipedia entries can be hijacked for self-serving or mischievous purposes.) Nor can we always be certain, when we Google for a particular piece of information, what the standpoint is of the Web site or blogger the search engine throws up. That's especially true of contentious topics such as Europe, immigration or the Middle East, but can apply to almost any subject. The Internet makes more information available than ever before; but more does not necessarily mean better. Google allows us not just to look up Gresham's Law ["bad money drives out good"], but also to experience it.

As a recovering journalist myself, I am not starry-eyed about the traditional media. False and mendacious stories abound. But there is also a lot of good, inquiring and rigorous journalism, or rather, there was. As we become more and more used to accessing free information via the Internet, we become less willing to pay for our news. And good journalism also tends to be expensive journalism: It takes time, and therefore money, to uncover truths that the powerful seek to hide. The less we are willing to pay for our news, the less proper journalism can be afforded.

There is one other disadvantage of the growth of the Internet. It makes it easier for each of us to discover only what we want to know and, increasingly, to pick out those facts and views that confirm our prejudices. I fear that soon we shall have far less of a shared understanding of our country and our world, and more of a narrower, more atomised outlook, as many of us use the new way of receiving news to avoid stories and viewpoints that challenge our outlook.

Take all those points together, and we can see why representative democracy can go either way. It might reinvent itself—or end up being destroyed.

Two Alternative Scenarios

Here are two alternative scenarios. First, reinvention. Politicians and officials realise that the new world requires not just the electronic distribution of the (expensive) paper documents they have churned out for years, it also requires greater candour, more explanation and more engagement. It requires a far greater flexibility, to accept that the Internet massively expands the ability of people to contribute to policy debates before final decisions are made—and (this is the trickiest bit) to acknowledge that this process will sometimes throw up better ideas than those emerging from Whitehall [shorthand for British government] advice or ministerial discussions.

The chances are that slowly ... the optimistic scenario will prevail. But we cannot be sure.

Reinvention also means accepting that direct democracy, or something close to it, is appropriate for some decisions, especially at the local level. I can see no reason these days why local residents shouldn't be far more intimately involved in decisions on such matters as planning applications and the installation (or removal) of road bumps.

All this involves a massive culture change—far removed from such risible displacement activities as online petitions. These prove nothing other than the levels of passion and organisation among obsessive minorities.

The alternative, pessimistic, scenario is that representative government ends up destroying itself. Politicians fail to adjust sensibly to the new world. They continue to decide in private,

E-Democracy Must Be Authentic, Not Convenient

Too often e-democracy has been promoted in the name of convenience: vote from bed, text message your MP [member of Parliament] while you're on the bus, press red buttons as a substitute for articulated opinion.... The elusive goal of democratic communication is not the quest for instantaneity, but the pursuit of mutual recognition. Democracy's problem is not its inability to synchronise touch-screen inputs and responsive outputs, in some cybernetic and populist fashion, but its failure to engender relationships of accountability, empathy and respect between representatives and represented. At its most democratic, representation entails an endeavour to mediate the presence of absent voices.

The democratic challenge for technology is not to simulate community or communion—the pretence of togetherness—but to help us deal with a world where we are never and can never be one and together. It is not reconnection that democracy needs most, but a healthy respect for the reality of disconnection. Technologies of instant connection are confidence tricks, like the White House Web site to which one can 'send a message to the president'. 'I think you're a lying trickster' says the message; 'The president thanks you so much for your message' says the almost-instant response. Authentic acknowledgement lies in the irregular, non-instant response, just as real music lies in the instrument that is not preprogrammed to have a perfectly regular beat.

Stephen Coleman and Jay G Blumler, The Internet and Democratic Citizenship: Theory, Practice and Policy, *New York: Cambridge University Press, 2009.*

engage too little and fail to heed the good ideas from outside the government process. They ignore the way the Internet is changing the seas in which they swim, or—worse—see this change as a threat to be repelled.

If that happens, then they will become more remote and out of touch; and as politics, like nature, abhors a vacuum, some new political force(s) will emerge to promise a greater direct say in big decisions. We have seen the beginnings of this in the rise of small, issue-based parties (some, like the Greens [an anti-capitalist, eco-friendly party], more attractive than others, such as the British National Party [a far-right, whites only party]). We have also seen the rise in promises of, and calls for far more, referendums. Add to this an era in which each of us tends to choose news that confirms our prejudices, and we have a recipe for a politics of anger and intolerance.

I hope that isn't the future we face; and, on balance, I don't think it is. The chances are that slowly—slower than is ideal—the optimistic scenario will prevail. But we cannot be sure. The pessimistic scenario is a real danger. Let us hope it does not prevail. Better, let us do what we can to ensure it doesn't.

How? I'd love to answer, but I have run out of space. In best, new-world manner, let's discuss it. What do you think?

Periodical Bibliography

The following articles have been selected to supplement the diverse views presented in this chapter.

Maria Bakardjieva	"Subactivism: Lifeworld and Politics in the Age of the Internet," *Information Society*, March 2009.
Economist	"The Perils of Modernity; The Internet and Malaysian Politics," March 15, 2008.
Daniel Finkelstein	"Come Down, Check It Out," *New Statesman*, March 19, 2009.
Rachel K. Gibson and Ian McAllister	"Does Cyber Campaigning Win Votes? Online Communication in the 2004 Australian Election," *Journal of Elections, Public Opinion, and Parties*, October 2006.
Vassia Gueorguieva	"Voters, MySpace, and YouTube," *Social Science Computer Review*, August 1, 2008.
Martin Hilbert	"The Maturing Concept of E-Democracy: From E-Voting and Online Consultations to Democratic Value Out of Jumbled Online Chatter," *Journal of Information Technology & Politics*, April 2009.
Evgeny Morozov	"Iran: Downside to the 'Twitter Revolution,'" *Dissent*, Fall 2009.
Fiona Ramsay	"The Politics of Social Media," *Marketing*, August 2009. www.marketingmagazine.co.uk.
Jeffrey W. Seifert and Jongpil Chung	"Using E-Government to Reinforce Government-Citizen Relationships," *Social Science Computer Review*, February 1, 2009.
Mitch Wagner	"Obama Election Ushering in First Internet Presidency," *Information Week*, November 5, 2008.

GLOBALVIEWPOINTS

Chapter 3

Internet Regulation and Censorship

Internet Filters in Australia Are Not Worth the Cost

Nick Farrell

According to Nick Farrell in the following viewpoint, national Internet filters to weed out bad Internet sites are pointless. While many countries such as Australia and Germany are signing up for mandatory filtering, the efficacy of such systems is questionable. Countries institute filtering to protect their citizens from offensive Web sites, but the sheer number of Web sites necessitates that the filters are forever changing to catch an increasing number of sites with offensive content. Additionally, an increasing number of sites that are not offensive will be banned by the filters as "false positives," Farrell argues. Those who want can often circumvent these filters, which renders suspect the entire idea of governments spending millions of dollars during a worldwide recession in a vain attempt to protect their citizens.

Farrell writes for IT News, an online news site.

As you read, consider the following questions:

1. According to the viewpoint, what is the chief reason Western nations advocate regulating which Web sites their citizens can view?

2. Why does Farrell claim that there will there be a substantial amount of false positives when filters attempt to identify bad material on the Internet?

Nick Farrell, "Opinion: Why National Internet Filters Are Pointless," itnews for Australian Business, January 22, 2009. Reproduced by permission of the author.

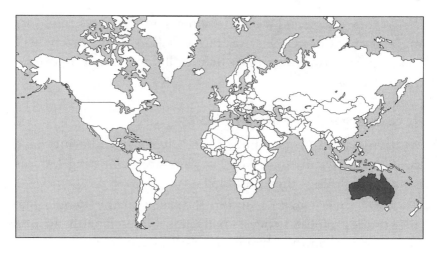

3. Why, according to Farrell, will filtering not stop purveyors of child pornography?

It seems that the world plus dog is falling over itself to filter the World Wide Web in a desperate bid to protect children from things they can handle on their own.

Australia, Germany and other so called free societies are signing up for mandatory filtering schemes.

The technology involved in such screening is similar to that tried more or less successfully in China and some of the more extreme religiously oriented countries.

It involves a list of sites that the government does not want its citizens to see being blocked at the ISP [Internet service provider].

Since this list requires much updating, the filtering software has a list of dodgy words that it does not like and will block pages containing those too.

Such country's creeds are against the individual and more in favour of state or religious stability being considered more important.

So they will spend a lot of money and resources monitoring and checking. Otherwise they will find their citizens will wake up and work out [that] they really don't want a government like that.

Reasons for State Regulation

Western nations which have been advocating filtering have done so solely on the basis that they are protecting kiddies from seeing things they shouldn't.

When they tend to mention the fact that they would like 'illegal sites' blocked they usually talk about it with hushed breath or mention the handy cover-all of terrorism.

Censorship is always about maintaining the status quo and keeping people ignorant.

However there is a fear that public servants will decide what is illegal and what information the great unwashed should see.

Censorship is always about maintaining the status quo and keeping people ignorant if that is threatened.

[Former British prime minister] Tony Blair would have loved to stick the phrase 'weapons of mass destruction' on any UK [United Kingdom] block list, for example.

But evidence from Australia seems to indicate that sticking such filtering at the ISP level either breaks the Internet or causes the whole thing to slow down to the days of dial-up modems.

Free speech issues are abstract but if you can't get your e-mails because the government is checking that you are not accessing porn then the Internet is in trouble.

This leads to another problem. Algorithms that are 99.999 per cent accurate in identifying 'bad' material might be technologically obtainable.

But with the huge numbers of Web pages going up every day you are still going to get a large number of false positives.

China has found that some of its more technology savvy minions have worked ways around its Great Fire Wall of China.

In the West, where the motivation towards censorship is not as fanatical, we suspect any filtering system will be cracked within minutes. Proxy servers, encryption and tunnelling are all tools that can and will be used.

Finally it will not actually stop paedophiles. The serious 'kiddie fiddler' Internet rings are extremely secure encrypted operations. Filtering won't even see the material they are shifting.

Yesterday [January 21, 2009] the Italian press was full of a story about Cathoogle.com which is a search engine set up by father Fortunato Di Noto, founder priest of [the] Meter [Association] who has been fighting kiddie porn for years.

Cathoogle.com was supposed to be a 'religiously correct' search engine with search words like 'sex', 'contraception', 'drugs' and 'abortion' not generating hits.

However on a slow news day rainnews24 hacks played around at the site and searched their way to all sorts of sites that would not have been approved of by the pope. This led to a somewhat unfair claim that paedophiles and pornographers have 'infiltrated' Cathoogle.com.

If a company with a limited Internet access point and a small number of users can't stop staff from going where they like, what chance does a government, with millions of users, . . . have?

Circumventing the System

There are companies out there which have been blocking staff access to some sites for years.

Objectionable Internet Material

The following table illustrates that categorizing objectionable Internet material is often problematic and not straightforward.

Child Pornography	Hate Speech	Pornography
• Society sees it as a problem.	• Society sees it as a problem.	• Society does *not* always see it as a problem.
• Child pornography is not a new problem.	• Racism and xenophobia are not new problems.	• Pornography is certainly *not* new.
• Digital child pornography is not a new problem—it can be traced back to the mid-1980s.	• Digital hate is not a new problem—it can be traced back to the mid-1980s.	• Difficult to categorize: Depending upon its nature and the laws of a specific State it could be considered illegal or harmful/offensive (*but* legal).
• Clear cut example of "illegal content".	• Difficult to categorize: Depending upon its nature and the laws of a specific State it could be considered illegal or harmful/offensive (*but* legal).	• Harm criteria are different in different European States.
• Criminalized by the CoE Cybercrime Convention, the UN Optional Protocol to the Convention on the Rights of the Child on the sale of children, child prostitution and child pornography, and the EU Council Framework Decision on combating the sexual exploitation of children and child pornography (not adopted yet).	• Harm criteria are different in different European States.	• UK approach is rather different to the German or Scandinavian approaches to sexually explicit content.
• **UN Optional Protocol: 108 signatories, 71 parties as of February 2004.**	• CoE Additional Protocol to the Cybercrime Convention on the criminalisation of acts of a racist and xenophobic nature committed through computer systems: **23 signatories so far but no ratifications.**	• **NO international attempt to regulate "sexually explicit content".**

Illegal ———————————————————————————————————————→ Legal

TAKEN FROM: Yaman Akdeniz, "Who Watches the Watchmen? The Role of Filtering Software in Internet Content Regulation," *The Media Freedom Internet Cookbook*, edited by Christian Möller and Arnaud Amouroux, Vienna: Organization for Security and Co-operation in Europe, 2004.

Firms find that employees will use a variety of high-tech and low-tech ways of getting around the filters.

Simple techniques such as going through a site such as Babel Fish with the translation set to English is surprisingly effective as is looking at the blocked site through Google cache.

That is even before staff start playing with proxy servicers.

If a company with a limited Internet access point and a small number of users can't stop staff from going where they like, what chance does a government, with millions of users, and a world load of Internet access points have?

Finally there will be the question of how much governments want to spend on Web filtering.

Some think it will only be a matter of a few hundred million and it will be sorted. China has spent a fortune and even that has been circumvented.

If the governments of Germany and Australia are prepared to keep paying for an unpopular system that will not do anything, in the middle of a recession, then they deserve to find out how pointless that is.

Japan's Internet Regulations May Create More Problems than They Solve

Chris Salzberg

As Japan moves to regulate the Internet, particularly by restricting the downloading of copyrighted material, numerous new problems are created, according to Chris Salzberg in the following viewpoint. Nebulous definitions of "content," "communications," and "downloading" make it difficult to decide exactly what material is intellectual property and what is not, he explains. While the goals of regulation are laudable, Salzberg questions whether the government can distinguish good content on the Internet from bad. He worries that regulation will limit freedom of speech, that the Japanese Internet will soon look very different, and that users will rue what they have lost.

Salzberg co-edits Global Voices, an international blog roundup, and also contributes to the Japan-based Web site Gyaku.jp.

As you read, consider the following questions:

1. According to Salzberg, what goals have motivated the Japanese government to regulate the Internet?
2. What is the problem with the concept of downloading, according to the viewpoint?

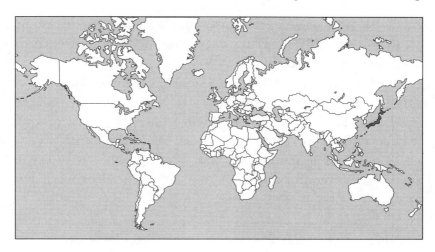

3. According to the author, how many comments did the government receive regarding its proposal to impose regulations on downloading?

In a country with one of the world's most vibrant Internet cultures, rumblings of change in the way that online information is managed, controlled and regulated is causing concern for many.

A series of reports and meetings last month [early in 2008] signaled a potentially far-reaching transformation in the legislative framework regulating Web access and file sharing in Japan. The transformation, should it happen, promises to bring to an end the days of the country's largely hands-off approach to online communication, ushering in an era of increased government involvement and heightened user liability.

New Regulations

On Dec. 6 [2007], the government released a final report, compiled by a study group set up by the Ministry of Internal Affairs and Communications, which set out plans to monitor and regulate the Internet in Japan. The proposed regulation targets all Web content, including online forms of traditional media such as newspaper articles and television broadcasting, while additionally covering user-generated content such as blogs and Web pages.

Days later, at a meeting on Dec. 10, the same ministry requested that mobile phone carriers NTT DoCoMo, KDDI, SoftBank and WILLCOM commence filtering Web access on mobile phones for users aged under 18. Responding to concerns over online dating sites, the filtering policy is broad in scope and covers forums, chat rooms and social network services.

Taken as a whole, these moves [toward regulation] reflect a shift in what authorities consider socially acceptable, and legally permissible, in the evolving realm of online interaction.

File sharing, meanwhile, was the topic discussed on Dec. 18 at a meeting of the Private Music and Video Recording Subcommittee of Japan's Agency for Cultural Affairs, a body under the Ministry of Education, Culture, Sports, Science and Technology. Authorities pushed for a ban on the downloading of copyrighted works (particularly music and videos) for private use, currently permitted under Japan's copyright law.

Taken as a whole, these moves reflect a shift in what authorities consider socially acceptable, and legally permissible, in the evolving realm of online interaction.

Lofty Goals

Motivated by lofty goals—upholding the common good, preserving safety and security, compensating creativity—attempts to rein in the disruptive nature of modern Web technologies nonetheless run counter to basic properties of online information.

Chief among these, and central to plans for regulation, is the assumption that online activity can be categorized.

Before the days of YouTube, "broadcast" was a term relegated in Japan to the transmission of television and radio, an area dominated by NHK [Japan Broadcasting Corporation] and major commercial TV and radio stations. Legislation of broadcast media historically strives to balance freedom of expression with the welfare of society as a whole.

Communication, on the other hand, historically meant point-to-point transmission via devices such as telephones. Legislation of this area prioritizes privacy and prohibition of censorship, aspects of communication critical at the level of the individual.

What happens, then, when the boundary between "broadcast" and "communication" becomes technologically obsolete?

This is the central issue addressed in the Dec. 6 report on Internet regulation, and it is a pressing one. While traditional media continue to hold powerful sway in Japan, the race is on to deliver content "all over IP" (all online), and Japan's powerful network infrastructure is already ready to handle it.

Redefining Boundaries

Against this background, the report sets out to define a legal framework unifying existing broadcast and telecommunications laws, endeavoring to apply elements of both realms to the Japanese Internet. It does so by categorizing online content under a series of headings—"media services," "special media services," "general media services," etc.—and legislates it accordingly, paralleling existing law where categories overlap.

Where the report classifies the content of Web services, however, serious concerns arise. Under the title of "kozensei" ("content that has openness"), for example, a wide range of currently unregulated services become eligible for forced content correction or removal. Blogs, Web pages, and bulletin board services such as popular Japanese forum 2channel all appear to fall in this group.

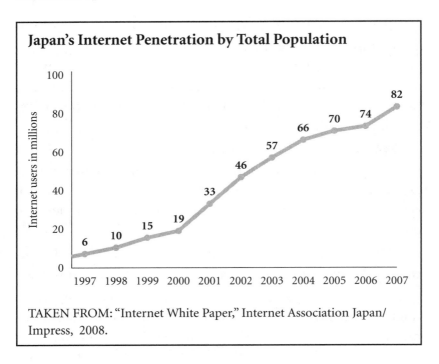

Japan's Internet Penetration by Total Population

TAKEN FROM: "Internet White Paper," Internet Association Japan/ Impress, 2008.

And yet the limits of the regulation are unclear, as the proposed categories, which borrow primarily from broadcast and telecommunications law, have little basis in the language of Web technology.

The limits of the regulation are unclear, as the proposed categories, which borrow primarily from broadcast and telecommunications law, have little basis in the language of Web technology.

Nico Nico Douga, for example, is a video sharing Web site, but it also acts as a kind of messaging service. Twitter is a messaging service, but is also a kind of blog; Mogo Mogo combines messaging and social networking functions. Boundaries on the Web are constantly being redefined, blurring the line between "broadcast" and "communication."

The Problem with Downloading

The proposed outlawing of "illegal downloads," coordinated by a different group under a separate ministry, faces a similar conundrum. Currently in Japan, while reproduction of copyrighted information is illegal, copies for "private use" are allowed. In their bid to make Japan a "nation built on intellectual property," government and industry groups are pushing to change this by revising Article 30 of Japan's copyright law, aiming to ban all downloads of copyrighted material.

The problem, however, is that everything on the Web is downloaded. Just to view a page, a browser must store its contents on the user's computer. Since it is impossible to know beforehand whether downloaded content is legal or not, any page view would, under the proposed revision, place the user at risk of violating copyright law.

Andreas Bovens, a Tokyo-based Belgian who blogs on copyright issues in Japan at Chosaq.net, sees a danger in this situation.

"It seems like the main targets of this proposed new legislation are Web sites offering unauthorized chaku-uta (ring tone) or music downloads," he says. "The message they seem to want to bring across is that downloading from those sites is illegal.

"However, although the scope of this legislation seems small, its effect is huge. It affects basically everything that we do on the Net [Internet]."

Stifling Freedom of Speech?

A similar tendency arises in the new filtering policy applied to mobile phones for underage users. In blocking access to Web sites considered dangerous to children, a net is thrown over the Web that snares a much wider range of content.

NTT DoCoMo, for example, has attracted criticism for filtering categories of content as sweeping as "lifestyles" (gay/lesbian), "religion," and "political activity." Classified under the heading of "communication," youth-oriented, game-download site Mobage [Town] meanwhile faces bankruptcy as a result of the filtering, which blocks half its user base.

Despite social and economic impacts, moves to regulate, manage and filter the Internet have attracted limited attention. Where there has been a response, it has mainly come through efforts on the part of active citizens and grassroots groups.

If citizens are robbed of their freedom on the Internet, then there is a risk that they will lose their capacity to make political choices.

A Japanese blogger who writes under the name of tokyodo-2005, and whose in-depth coverage motivated many citizens to submit public comments to the government in response to planned Web regulation, argues that the government is attempting to stifle freedom of speech.

"This is a country where people have been detained for days just for distributing flyers," he says. "If citizens are robbed of their freedom on the Internet, then there is a risk that they will lose their capacity to make political choices."

Inevitable Change

The proposal to outlaw illegal downloads also attracted a response coordinated partly through Movements for the Internet Active Users (MIAU), a group established last October to raise awareness about the development and regulation of Web technology in Japan. Masayuki Hatta is one of MIAU's original members.

"While regulation targets the negative sides of the Internet, there are positives to the Web as well," he explains. "It has become a new space for innovation and creativity. They want to regulate the Net because of its negative side, but the way they are going about this is wrong, and the voices of users are not being heard. We wanted to do something about this."

Yet while the government received more than 8,000 public comments—a relatively high number—largely opposing the proposed download policy, officials have described the revision of copyright law as "inevitable."

Internet regulation in other areas is similarly moving ahead apace. Administrators plan to submit a bill on the unification of broadcast and communications laws to the regular Diet session [Japanese legislature] in 2010. Default Web filtering on mobile phones for minors starts this year.

With all these changes, the Japanese Internet—the future medium of communication in Japan—may come out looking very different. Sadly, it may only be once this happens that its users, looking back with the benefit of hindsight, appreciate what they once had—and what they lost.

Gaza's People Need Support from the Western World to Preserve Their Internet Freedom

Niv Lillian and Nir Boms

In this viewpoint, Niv Lillian and Nir Boms write that in the war-torn Gaza Strip, Islamic terrorists regularly bomb Internet cafes, which they consider havens for pornography and other unholy pastimes. This is ironic in that these same terrorists make use of the Internet to promote their own evil operations. The Internet is an indispensible tool in Gaza that is often the only way for residents to enjoy the basic freedom to connect with the rest of the world. The authors call for the Western world to support the people of Gaza, speak out against terrorist censors, and not allow terrorists to take away access to the moderate voices in and outside of Gaza.

Lillian is the deputy editor of Ynet's Computers and Internet channel; Boms is vice president of the Center for Freedom in the Middle East.

As you read, consider the following questions:

1. According to the e-mail from the "Islamic Swords of Justice," why did they bomb the Internet cafe in Gaza?

2. How do terrorist organizations such as al Qaeda use the Internet, in the authors' view?

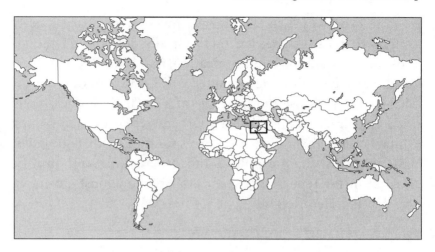

3. What, according to the viewpoint, is the "potent outcome" of such attacks?

At 3 am, in the shadow of the ongoing fighting, a giant blast shook Allah al-Shawa's Internet cafe in Gaza. The owner, who rushed to his business in order to examine the damage, found one computer in working order in the rubble and decided to check his e-mail.

A surprise awaited him: An e-mail message from a group calling itself "Islamic Swords of Justice" explained that the cafe was blown up because it and those of its type "divert the attention of an entire generation to other issues that are not jihad or worship." In other words, the e-mail charged that his Internet cafe was used for distributing abomination and pornography.

Violent Censorship

Al-Shawa is not alone. Since December [2006], in the framework of the anarchy that has taken root in the Gaza Strip, various radical groups have blown up dozens of Internet cafes alongside attacks on Christian bookstores and other sites associated with Western culture, such as music shops and pool halls.

The groups, which intelligence investigators have loosely connected to al Qaeda, are methodically eliminating the almost sole means of communication that Gaza's 1.4 million residents have with the outside world. Students at the al-Azhar University use the Internet cafes for their studies, along with academicians and civilians just interested in maintaining contacts with their relatives, corresponding with colleagues, and generally maintaining a life of creation and prolific thought of the type that is safely available to almost anyone in the Western Hemisphere.

Terror is the quickest way to a monopoly in the market of ideas.

As opposed to regimes such as Iran and Syria, which engage in censorship through government orders and technological monitoring means reminiscent of the Orwellian thought police [author George Orwell's conceptions of social injustice], marginal groups such as the "Islamic Swords of Justice" utilize much simpler censorship means: dynamite sticks. Yet there is a common pattern to the dark regimes and no less fundamentalist explosive cells: sowing fear, horror, and restraint among citizens. Terror is the quickest way to a monopoly in the market of ideas.

The Poor Pay the Heaviest Price

The irony inherent in this absurd situation is doubly bitter: Those who consume pornography online usually do it in the privacy of their own homes and not in the public space of a cafe because of the shame and the religious code that condemns such conduct. Therefore, those who really suffer from the attacks are the people who cannot afford a computer or regular Internet connection at their homes—that is, students and other poor segments of society.

During . . . the recent Lebanon war and within the walls of the besieged Gaza Strip, in recent years we saw bloggers and brave Internet activists with a thirst for dialogue with the other side, who did not shy away from criticizing even those who control their Internet connection. They, the supporters of globalization, indeed constitute a threat to reactionary Islamic forces, which would go to any length in order to silence these opponents.

The second irony is the paradox inherent in the approach of Islamic zealots to the Internet, a tool they widely utilize in order to issue religious edicts, produce video broadcasts from al Qaeda headquarters, and communicate among terror activists.

For example, the "Tawhid and Jihad Brigades" sent an e-mail where it claimed to have executed BBC reporter Alan Johnston, abducted in Gaza about two months ago [in early 2007]. Al-Shawa explains this theater of the absurd: "They use the Internet in order to spread their message, yet assume that everyone else uses the Internet to get porn."

This attack on the virtual space is not only limited to [undermining] the livelihood of al-Shawa and his colleagues, who make a living from operating Internet cafes. The cutting of a modern line of communication such as the Internet is no less severe than hitting other basic infrastructure such as electricity or water.

The Western world must not remain silent in the face of such basic attacks on freedom of expression.

The West Must Not Remain Silent

The potent outcome of such attacks is immense: The cutting off of the main pipeline that brings ideas of freedom and equality into the besieged [Gaza] Strip prevents the popula-

Afghanistan's Taliban Uses and Abuses the Internet

In August 2001, the Taliban outlawed the use of the Internet in Afghanistan, except at the fundamentalist group's headquarters. The Taliban, nevertheless, maintained a prominent home on the Internet despite United Nations sanctions, retaliatory hack attacks, and the vagaries of the United States bombing campaign. The unofficial Web site of Dharb-I-Mu'min, an organisation named by the United States on a list of terrorist groups, is still operational. Another site, entitled Taliban Online, contained information including instructions on how to make financial donations, or donations of food and clothing, to the Afghan militia, but is no longer operational. In addition, a United States-based Web site operated by the group was shut down in late September 2001 following a request from the United States Treasury Department to the group's Kansas City-based ISP [Internet service provider].

One of the larger *jihad*-related sites still in operation is Azzam.com. . . . The Azzam site is available in more than a dozen languages and offers primers including 'How Can I Train Myself for Jihad.' A number of Azzam's affiliates were shut down after people complained to the ISPs hosting the sites. . . . The British company Swift Internet, which was the technical and billing contact for an Azzam site, is said to have received threatening e-mails accusing it of supporting a terrorist Web site. Swift has since distanced itself from the site by removing its name as a contact on public Internet records. Meanwhile, as often as the site is shut down, it is replaced by a substitute/mirror site under a different URL. Said the Azzam spokesperson: "One cannot shut down the Internet."

Maura Conway, "Reality Bytes:
Cyberterrorism and Terrorist 'Use' of the Internet,"
Trinity College, 2002. http://doras.dcu.ie.

tion from opening its eyes and aspiring for such values. Instead, it is fed by ongoing ideological calls for jihad against Western infidels.

The Western world must not remain silent in the face of such basic attacks on freedom of expression. We, citizens of the liberal world, tend to forget this, but freedom of expression is also freedom of thought and the freedom to listen to new ideas—a basic liberty that religious zealots have wrested away from Gaza residents.

We too, as Israelis, have a clear interest in maintaining Gaza's virtual space. The rubble of Internet cafes, just like Gaza's rubble in general, does not bring us closer to a time of calm.

This happens while the moderates and brave figures on the other side are met with a wall of disconnection from that same space that could have allowed for dialogue. Without advancing the principles of freedom and equality, and without the free distribution of ideas and information through a robust communication infrastructure, there is certainly no hope for moderate voices of sanity.

Cubans Need Unrestricted Internet Access

Rogelio Vilarreal

In the viewpoint that follows, Rogelio Vilarreal marvels at the changes that technology has brought the world in the last half century. Jobs such as those his father made a living at have been rendered obsolete in this high-tech world. However, technology has good and bad uses. Many governments use new technologies to suppress freedom of speech, Vilarreal says, and limit what information their people can access. Cuba is a well-known perpetrator of such policies, as is China. In Vilarreal's view, the Cuban people deserve unregulated access to one of the world's great technological marvels, the Internet.

Vilarreal is the author of El dilema de Bukowski *(Bukowski's Dilemma)* and *El periodismo cultural en los tiempos de la globalifobia* (Cultural Journalism in the Times of Global Phobia). *He is editor in chief of* Replicante *magazine. He lives in Mexico, where he is well known as a counterculture figure.*

As you read, consider the following questions:

1. According to Vilarreal, what type of work did his father do and how has technology made it obsolete?
2. Why has Cuba been named an enemy of the Internet by the organization Reporters Without Borders?
3. What types of pictures are featured on Yoani Sánchez's Web site Generación Y?

Rogelio Vilarreal, "The Digital Century," zonezero.com, August 2008. Reproduced by permission of the author.

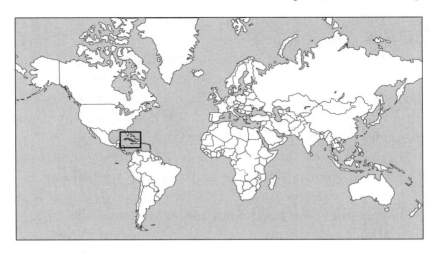

Fifty years ago, when I was born, the world of the late 20th and early 21st centuries was unconceivable, even in the most far-fetched sci-fi movies. It is not the comfy fun world of [sixties animated sitcom] *The Jetsons* nor the catastrophe depicted in [American film] *Planet of the Apes*, but a more complex and engaging one, closer to the one foreseen in [Ridley Scott's] *Blade Runner* in 2019 Los Angeles or, unfortunately the one portrayed in a desperate New York City in [American film] *Soylent Green*.

Technology Has Changed the World

Nowadays, the overwhelming technological and scientific advancements taking place in every aspect of our lives are a commonplace for the younger generations, who for evident reasons have a better access to these advancements. Millions of children and teenagers can't conceive a world without iPods, cell phones with cameras and GPS [global positioning system], chat rooms, social networks and online games that grow in sophistication by the day. Certainly, they would not enjoy as much a film that does not feature all those spectacular digital special effects. Needless to say, the transformations of education, art, journalism and research that have been brought on by the worldwide endless virtual hyper-library would amaze [Argentine writer Jorge Luis] Borges himself, even though he somehow foretold it in his [short story] "The Aleph." Man's arrival to the moon in 1969 and the recent discovery of the human genome—just to mention a couple of major scientific breakthroughs—would have been impossible to achieve without digital technology.

There was no TV—not even a black and white model—in my parents' house until the mid-60s and a telephone (oh wonder of wonders!) until a few years later. The yellowish family pictures were kept in thick black cardboard albums; my first school assignments were typed in a modern Olivetti machine. Time and time again, I had to consult historical dates and names in my dad's library.

In some countries, the loathing towards democracy has led some governments to ban the use of the Internet to the population, and even watch and harass them using this medium.

Now that I've mentioned my father, he worked as a linotype machine operator, copywriter and editor. So what in the world is a linotype? The linotype is kind of a huge typing machine with a bucket filled with melted lead that was used in the printing process of books, magazines and newspapers. Nowadays it belongs in a museum, such as the one exhibited in Mexico City's publishing house Fondo de Cultura Económica. In this day and age, printing is made with silent offset machines that are the size of an 18-wheeler, using a computer. A laptop with editing software is all you need to design a publication.

Long gone are the huge worktables, all the cutting and pasting made by hand, and so are the cumbersome photo-editing machines resembling the contraptions created by the mad scientists of the campy Santo movies of yesteryear. Nowadays, we don't have to take mechanical originals to the printers, we can send the text via e-mail, no matter if the publishing house is in Hong Kong or Shanghai. . . .

Anything that happened before the digital era is ancient history for the children and teens that have grown up and been educated in the digital technology environment. The use of digital technology such as computers and the Internet is a natural thing for them. Links and hypertext reflect the way in which the human brain and nonlinear thinking work, simultaneously processing images, concepts and jumping from one subject to the other, going back or forward in time and space, either intentionally or by free association, very much like surfing the Web.

Good and Bad Uses of Technology

Digital technology is also used for espionage, war and destruction. In this sense, the world is no better than before. In some countries, the loathing towards democracy has led some governments to ban the use of the Internet to the population, and even watch and harass them using this medium, as the Chinese government did to the blogs of dissident writers Tsering Woeser and Wang Lixiong for speaking in favor of Tibet's independence. "The couple has been under house arrest since the beginning of the riots [in] March [of 2008]"— reported Mexican writer Eve Gil—and continues: "The censorship in the Internet has spread to SMS [short message service] messaging with the collaboration (or complicity?) of companies such as Yahoo and Google. China has the best filtering and censorship system in the world, and has used it to incarcerate at least 50 people."

Another example of a blatant disregard to freedom of speech takes place in Cuba, where a very small part of the population owns a computer and has Internet access. A report of the organization Reporters Without Borders states that:

Although it is true that there are problems to go online in Cuba, it is hard to believe that www.desdecuba.com has had to deal with technical difficulties for ten years. These kinds of restrictions go against the recent government measures to facilitate the access of Cubans to mass media, including the Internet. One cannot exist without the other. The signs of openness given by Raúl Castro's government should include more respect for freedom of speech.

Since March 20th 2008, the Web site www.desdecuba.com cannot be accessed from public places such as cybercafes or hotels. The very few private connections used for professional reasons or clandestinely, take at least 20 minutes to load the home page. Making comments is practically impossible.

The Internet is fiercely controlled by the state. There is a single network that can be accessed to send e-mails abroad, but it does not allow [users] to surf the Web, according to the report of Reporters Without Borders: "Access to the Internet is three times more expensive and it allows [users] to visit foreign news Web sites, such as the BBC, *Le Monde* or the *El Nuevo Herald* (a Miami-based newspaper written in Spanish), but if an address such as "google.fr" is typed, one is redirected to the Web page of Cuba's official newspaper *Granma* or the Prensa Latina news agency."

It is deplorable that millions of Chinese and Cubans do not have unrestricted access to the most important information, education and entertainment network in human history.

Cuba Is an "Enemy of the Internet"

Not surprisingly, Cuba is on the list of "Enemies of the Internet" published by Reporters Without Borders, on March 12, 2008.

Cuba Is Among the Internet's "Black Holes"

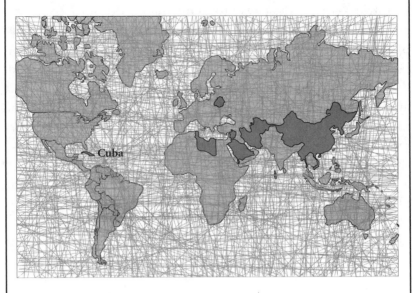

Fifteen countries are "black holes" in the World Wide Web, according to
Reporters Without Borders: Belarus, Burma, China, Cuba, Iran, Libya, Maldives, Nepal,
North Korea, Saudi Arabia, Syria, Tunisia, Turkmenistan, Uzbekistan, and Vietnam.

TAKEN FROM: Reporters Without Borders for Press freedom.
www.rsf.org.

One of Cuba's . . . most popular Web sites, which has received the 2008 Ortega y Gasset Award of digital journalism is Generación Y. Written by young author Yoani Sánchez, it comments on the everyday life of Castro's island, featuring sad pictures of run-down buildings, policemen arresting homosexuals, broken-down electricity meters and the temporary joys of the carnival. Ironically, Yoani does not have a computer in her own home.

Digital technology and its advantages are not for everyone, in spite of its rapid growth. In this sense, it is deplorable that millions of Chinese and Cubans do not have unrestricted access to the most important information, education and entertainment network in human history, but also that millions of people in Africa and Latin America that live in democratic countries—or on their way to democracy—do not have access either, due to poverty, unemployment and the lack of policies of education and scientific and technological development. Digital technology can make a positive change in the world, but it can only flourish in an environment of freedom, respect and prosperity. We have been through enough wars. If the media are extensions of man—as [former University of Toronto professor and media expert Marshall] McLuhan put it— the new technologies should be at the service of the growth and peaceful development of every man and woman on the planet.

Europe Must Preserve an Open Internet

Cory Doctorow

In this viewpoint, Cory Doctorow urges the European Union not to enact a new telecommunications package that will give Internet service providers the ability to exercise more control over the Internet. The real victims of such a law will be start-up companies that are in the same place that Google was in the late 1990s. Excessive control by the service providers will crush innovation and experimentation, which have been catalysts for the Internet since its inception. The telecommunications companies that offer Internet service, which have benefitted from public subsidies, must not be allowed to turn on the taxpayers and countries that have supported them. If they don't appreciate the system as it is now constructed, Doctorow writes, other companies will surely be happy to take their places and ensure a more open Internet.

Doctorow is a science fiction author, activist, journalist and blogger. He is the co-editor of BoingBoing.net and the author of the novel Little Brother. *He is the former European director of the Electronic Frontier Foundation and co-founded the Open Rights Group.*

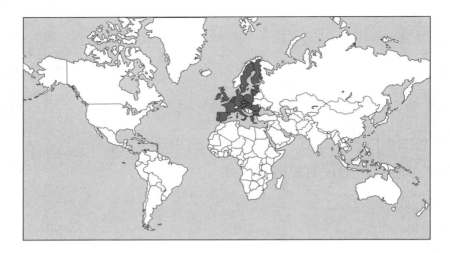

As you read, consider the following questions:

1. According to Cory Doctorow, what are some of the ways in which Internet service providers (ISPs) are "pulling the rug out" from under those who have supported them?

2. According to the viewpoint, why aren't giant companies such as Google and Yahoo likely to be victims of network discrimination?

3. According to Doctorow, how does metering Internet usage discourage experimentation?

If politicians want to effect economic recovery, national competitiveness, good public health and high civic engagement, they have a duty to keep the Internet free and open. But politicians around the world seem willing to sacrifice their national interest to keep a few powerful phone and telcoms companies happy.

Take the Telcoms Package now before the EU: Among other things, the package paves the way for ISPs and Quangos to block or slow access to Web sites and services on an arbitrary basis. At the same time, ISPs are instituting and enforcing strict bandwidth limits on their customers, citing shocking statistics about the bandwidth hogs who consume vastly more resources than the average punter.

Between filtering, fiddling connection speeds and capping usage, ISPs are pulling the rug out from under the nations that have sustained them with generous subsidies and regulation.

Take filtering: By allowing ISPs to silently block access to sites that displease them, we invite all the ills that accompany censorship—Telus, a Canadian telcom that blocked access to a site established by its striking workers where they were airing their grievances. Around the world, ISPs co-operate with censorious governments in their mission to keep their citizens in the dark: For example, ISPs in the United Arab Emirates are blocking access to stories about a UAE royal family member who was video-recorded torturing a merchant with whom he had a business dispute. As a matter of policy, Transport for London isn't allowed to block us from riding the tube to a rally in support of striking transit workers; British Gas doesn't turn our heat off if they suspect we're housing a benefits cheat; and BT doesn't divert our phone calls if we're ringing up a competitor to change carriers. Giving an ISP censorship powers—and then layering censorship in secrecy and arbitrariness—we make the Internet a less trustworthy and less useful place to be.

The real victims of network discrimination are the nimble little start-ups, the firms that are in the same position today that Google was in 10 years ago.

ISPs would also like to be able to arbitrarily slow or degrade our network connections depending on what we're doing and with whom. In the classic "traffic shaping" scenario, a company like Virgin Media strikes a deal with Yahoo to serve its videos on a preferential basis, and then slows its customers' connections to Google, Hulu, and other video-hosting sites to ensure that Virgin's videos are the quickest to load. As the Craigslist founder, Craig Newmark, said, this is like the phone company putting you on hold when you ring your local pizzeria, with a message inviting you to press one to be immediately connected to Domino's, its "preferred pizza partner".

But the real action in network fiddling isn't the battle between giants such as Yahoo and Google. Both well-established, have armies of otherwise unoccupied "business development" people lying around, and are handily capable of fanning out across the globe and buying lunch for their opposite numbers at every telcoms operator on the planet. The real victims of network discrimination are the nimble little start-ups, the firms that are in the same position today that Google was in 10 years ago when it consisted of a few marginally funded hackers and some taped-together hardware under a desk.

Google needn't be the last Google. It needn't be the last firm to emerge from the fevered imagination of two bright kids and turn the world on its ear. And it need not always come from Silicon Valley. Just as Research In Motion was able to take the world by storm from Waterloo, Ontario; just as Moo.com was able to conquer the world's business-card needs from Clerkenwell, so, too could the next remarkable start-up emerge from the UK.

Unless, that is, the cost of entry into the market goes up by four or five orders of magnitude, growing to encompass the cost of a horde of glad-handing negotiators who must first secure the permission of gatekeepers at the telcoms giants. In that case, only the least experimental, safest, lowest-risk/lowest-return firms will be capitalized, because no one wants to take a big plunge on a risky proposition that could be stopped dead in its tracks by a phone company that's already given pole position to an incumbent.

Finally, there's the question of metered billing for ISP customers. The logic goes like this: "You have a 20Mbs connection, but if you use that connection as though it were unmetered, you will saturate our bandwidth and everyone will suffer." ISPs like to claim that their caps are "fair" and that the majority of users fit comfortably beneath them, and that only a tiny fraction of extraordinary bandwidth hogs reach the ceiling.

The reality is that network usage follows a standard statistical distribution, the "Pareto distribution," a power-law curve in which the most active users are exponentially more active than the next-most-active group, who are exponentially more active than the next group, and so on. This means that even if you kick off the 2% at the far right-hand side of the curve, the new top 2% will continue to be exponentially more active than the remainder. Think of it this way: There will always be a group of users in the "top 2%" of bandwidth consumption. If you kick those users off, the next-most-active group will then be at the top. You can't have a population that doesn't have a ninety-eighth percentile.

But the real problem of per-usage billing is that no one—not even the most experienced Internet user—can determine in advance how much bandwidth they're about to consume before they consume it. Before you clicked on this article, you had no way of knowing how many bytes your computer would consume before clicking on it. And now that you've clicked on it, chances are that you still don't know how many bytes you've consumed. Imagine if a restaurant billed you by the number of air molecules you displaced during your meal, or if your phone bills varied on the total number of syllables you uttered at 2dB or higher.

Even ISPs aren't good at figuring this stuff out. Users have no intuition about their bandwidth consumption and precious little control over it.

Metering usage discourages experimentation. If you don't know whether your next click will cost you 10p or £2, you will become very conservative about your clicks. Just look at the old AOL, which charged by the minute for access, and saw that very few punters were willing to poke around the many offerings its partners had assembled on its platform. Rather, these people logged in for as short a period as possible and logged off when they were done, always hearing the clock ticking away in the background as they worked.

This is good news for incumbents who have already established their value propositions for their customers, but it's a death sentence for anything new emerging on the Net.

Between these three factors—reducing the perceived value of the Net, reducing the ability of new entrants to disrupt incumbents, and penalizing those who explore new services on the Net—we are at risk of scaring people away from the network, of giving competitive advantage to firms in better-regulated nations, of making it harder for people to use the Net to weather disasters, to talk to their government and to each other.

Telcoms companies argue that their responsibility is to their shareholders, not the public interest, and that they are only taking the course of maximum profitability. It's not their business to ensure that the Googles of tomorrow attain liftoff from the garages in which they are born.

We are at risk of scaring people away from the network, . . . of making it harder for people to use the Net to weather disasters, to talk to their government and to each other.

But telcoms firms are all recipients of invaluable public subsidy in the form of rights of way and other grants that allow them to string their wires over and under our streets and through our homes. You and I can't go spelunking in the sewers with a spool of cable to wire up our own alternative network. And if the phone companies had to negotiate for every pole, every sewer, every punch-down, every junction box, ev-

European Threats to Internet Privacy

In Europe, the surveillance of traffic data is not yet focused on copyright infringement policies, but it soon will be, and when combined with antiterrorism policies, it could be disastrous. Currently various governments in the European Union [EU] are establishing national policies that compel communications service providers . . . to *retain* their traffic data logs. Under previous law, these service providers would have to delete this personal information once it was no longer necessary. . . . Now in countries like Italy, France, and the United Kingdom [UK], service providers will have to retain this information regarding users' e-mail, Internet and telephone habits . . . for periods ranging between one and five years. The UK, France, Ireland and Sweden are also pushing for this policy to be adopted at the EU, thus obliging all countries to compel all communications providers throughout Europe to keep this information for a number of years, just in case one day this information is of value to law enforcement authorities.

The surveillance of subscriber and traffic data is tantamount to the collection and tracking of all human conduct in the Information Society: who we speak with, who we move with, what we look for, where we receive information from, and where we send it to. As a result of these policies, European users of the Internet will have to grow accustomed to the idea that their actions will be logged for a number of years and accessible to any government that is interested, and possibly others.

Gus Hosein, "Future Challenges of the Information Society,"
The Media Freedom Internet Cookbook,
edited by Christian Möller and Arnaud Amouroux, Vienna:
Organization for Security and Co-operation in Europe, 2004.

ery road they get to tear up, they'd go broke. All the money in the world couldn't pay for the access they get for free every day.

If they don't like it, they don't have to do it. But we don't have to give them our sewers and streets and walls, either. Governments and regulators are in a position to demand that these recipients of public subsidy adhere to a minimum standard of public interest. If they don't like it, let them get into another line of work—give them 60 days to get their wires out of our dirt and then sell the franchise to provide network services to a competitor who will promise to give us a solid digital future in exchange for our generosity.

Network Neutrality May Not Be Practical

Bill Thompson

According to Bill Thompson in the following viewpoint, the Internet is in danger of taxing its infrastructure to the point where there will not be enough bandwidth to carry the load of all the data-intensive applications that are being developed. New Web applications are often heavy on sound and video, and send large amounts of data over the Internet. With more users coming online all the time, Thompson explains, the system may reach the point where fast, reliable service begins to decline. The concept of net neutrality, which argues that all corporations and citizens pay the same amount to use the Internet, regardless of how much bandwidth they consume, may need rethinking. Net neutrality is a desirable concept, but it may soon become outdated, Thompson argues.

Thompson is a writer who appears regularly on Digital Planet *and writes for the BBC News Web site.*

As you read, consider the following questions:

1. How many megabytes does the data-intensive application Joost use, according to the viewpoint?
2. According to Phil Smith of Cisco Systems, how much data can routers handle?
3. According to Thompson, what "correction" may be necessary to fix the data overload problem?

During the first months of 2007 a select few million people were fortunate enough to be offered early access to Joost, a Web site that delivers high-quality video over the Internet, developed by Niklas Zennström and Janus Friis.

The duo, also behind online telephony provider Skype, are signing up content providers for the official launch of their new offering later this year [in 2007], and the feeling is that it could do as much damage to the business models of commercial television providers as Skype did to traditional telecoms [telecommunications] companies, forcing them to offer VoIP (voice over Internet protocol) services, and reducing their revenues in the process.

Joost's real impact, however, may be felt elsewhere. In order to deliver high-quality, full-screen video it has to pump vast amounts of data over the Internet, and experts such as Eric Openshaw, principal and leader of the Technology, Media & Telecommunications practice at Deloitte America, fear the network may not be able to take the strain.

Joost downloads about 320 megabytes of data per hour, and the peer-to-peer model it uses means that each viewer is also sending up to 150 megabytes to other users, the equivalent of 50 iTunes songs.

Joost is not the only high-bandwidth service targeting home users. BT Vision, the Internet TV service from BT [formerly British Telecommunications], requires fast connectivity, as do popular video chat services offered by Yahoo, Microsoft and Apple. Games players who plug their consoles into the network for interactive play on Microsoft's Xbox LIVE or Sony's PlayStation Network expect fast responses and reliable links, while the millions of people uploading and downloading videos from YouTube or putting photos on Flickr, Photobucket, MySpace and Facebook are quick to complain if the network slows down or their connection is lost.

Businesses Are Heavy Bandwidth Users

Businesses have long been heavy bandwidth users, and new services will add further pressure. Thousands of small firms are adopting online collaborative tools such as Basecamp to manage projects, or Amazon's S3 (simple storage service), to host data online instead of running their own servers. Some are even off-loading their entire IT [information technology] infrastructure, from e-mail to word processing, onto Google.

These services [NetMeeting, Skype and WebEx] all depend on fast, reliable networks, and can use a lot of bandwidth when large files are being shared.

Simon Appleton, the Brighton-based entrepreneur who founded the successful online recruitment service PlanetRecruit, is now CEO [chief executive officer] of job search engine Workcircle. His small team uses a variety of online tools, including Central Desktop for sharing documents and Campfire to host virtual meetings, keeping the need for office attendance to a minimum.

The same is true at Cambridge-based data protection company nCipher. CEO Alex van Someren says the firm uses collaborative and IP-based [Internet protocol-based] tools such as NetMeeting, Skype and WebEx regularly "to minimise travel and maximise productivity". These services all depend on fast, reliable networks, and can use a lot of bandwidth when large files are being shared.

The Net [Internet] is also used to maintain contact with customers and van Someren admits his company is "strongly dependent on good Internet bandwidth to maintain our dialogue with customers, employees and partners". Simon Appleton points out that "as a distributed company, we need the network for both external and internal communication, as well as the operation of our Web site, which is our business".

Sufficient Capacity—or Not?

It might seem there is more than enough capacity on the Internet to meet even the most ambitious projections for growth. New fibre-optic links are being installed to extend the "long-haul" backbones that move data between cities, countries and continents, and breakthroughs in signal transmission hold out the prospect of faster data speeds.

The Internet2 project, a university-led research consortium developing new network technologies, has announced a 100 gigabit per second link between Washington[, D.C.] and New York, sufficient to download a DVD movie every second. This is an astonishing technical achievement and one which indicates that we are unlikely to be short of backbone bandwidth.

But fast backbones may not be enough. Other network components must also work harder. In February 2007, an attack on the servers that keep track of computer names, the Domain Name System, slowed the whole network significantly and the routers, which direct data around the network, require constant upgrades to keep up with traffic growth.

It's largely a problem of capacity. At the end of every high-speed cable there needs to be a switch that looks at each of the billions of data "packets" being transmitted to decide where it goes next. The Internet is a vast collection of connected networks, and the routers decide how data flows efficiently between them.

Keeping up with network growth poses a serious challenge to companies like Cisco Systems, which manufactures the routers that glue the network together. Speaking recently to the BBC, Phil Smith, Cisco's head of technology and corporate [marketing] said: "Routers have come a long way. Those we're talking about now can handle 92 terabits per second. We have enough capacity to do that and drive a billion phone calls from those same people who are playing a video game at the same time as they're having a text chat."

Cisco's confident assertions won't mollify everyone. Alex van Someren of nCipher is concerned about new services, pointing out that "the growth in spam, VoIP and video social networking sites is chewing up bandwidth at an accelerating pace." His concern is that today's Web 2.0 services require more than simply sending Web pages to clients. Services like Google Maps continuously exchange data between the user's browser and Google's map server, and this, too, is straining the network.

The end result is that users notice when the connection slows down, because the mapping service stutters and the near-instant response time becomes a few seconds, breaking the illusion of a seamless and real-time interaction. This isn't just an irritant to baseball-capped home gamers. Delays in updating a shared, online whiteboard can severely disrupt a business meeting, while pixellation or lost audio in a critical video conference could jeopardise a deal.

The Potential for Data Overload

There's potential for a major overload, too. Andrew Coburn is vice president of catastrophe research at Risk Management Solutions, which provides risk assessment for insurance and financial companies. He says that while we can cope at current traffic levels, an external event like a terrorist attack or a flu pandemic could easily overload today's strained network.

"A massive increase in traffic that resulted in overloads of router buffers and caused localised and progressive failure through the network is one of our major concerns," he warns. "Packet loss leads to degradation of service, increased waiting times and reduces reliability to the point of unusability."

There isn't enough information to determine how real the risk is. "Each of the many thousands of individual service providers knows their own demand-supply relationships and the reliability that they expect," adds Coburn. "But these data are not public, and each sees only their own small part of the

Network Neutrality Treats All Internet Activity Equally

Network neutrality [net neutrality] is best defined as a network design principle. The idea is that a maximally useful public information network aspires to treat all content, sites, and platforms equally. This allows the network to carry every form of information and support every kind of application. The principle suggests that information networks are often more valuable when they are *less* specialized. . . .

A useful way to understand this principle is to look at other networks, like the electric grid, which are implicitly built on a neutrality theory. . . . The electric grid does not care if you plug in a toaster, an iron, or a computer. Consequently, it has survived and supported giant waves of innovation in the appliance market. The electric grid worked for the radios of the 1930s [and] works for the flat screen TVs of the 2000s.

Tim Wu, "Network Neutrality FAQ,"
Timwu.org, 2009. www.timwu.org.

overall network. Nobody has more than a glimpse into the total network that comprises today's Internet."

Fast, reliable backbone links and a new generation of routers supporting network protocols designed to make traffic flow more efficiently may solve the long-haul problem, but they do little to tackle the "last mile", the distance between the high-speed backbone and the end user. In April [2007], telecoms regulator Ofcom reported that over half of UK [United Kingdom] adults now have a broadband Internet connection from home, with an average speed of just under four megabytes per second. It also found that 29 per cent of them are listening to online audio, and 26 per cent are watching video at least once a week. And over half of us are now also making phone calls over the Internet.

The rapid rise in domestic Internet use is an opportunity for businesses to trade online, but it also creates problems, especially for small businesses connected to the network using the same ADSL (asymmetric digital subscriber line) or cable links offered to home users. Larger companies are more likely to have dedicated data connections over leased lines or even fibre. nCipher has one permanent, high-speed, leased line and one ADSL backup line at each major trading location, while Workcircle relies solely on ADSL.

Limiting network use is a short-term solution; providers need incentives to change their offerings.

One indication that ISPs (Internet service providers) are aware of the problem is the introduction of data capping and "bandwidth shaping," where the capacity of a connection is temporarily reduced to help manage demand. In the UK, Virgin Media has started doing this, as has AT&T in the United States.

But limiting network use is a short-term solution; providers need incentives to change their offerings. According to Appleton, "it's time for ISPs to stop hiding behind caveats about speed, and stop tying us into long contracts." He believes that once customers can move more easily between suppliers then the pressure will be on to find better solutions.

The network is not going to fall over, at least not unless we have a disaster of the scale of the 2006 earthquake in the Indian Ocean that severed nine undersea cables and cut most of southern China off from the Internet for several days. But the assumption that ISPs will deliver the bandwidth they promise is now questionable. And businesses that rely on fast, trouble-free network access should be aware of the risks.

The Problem with Net Neutrality

The days of cheap and plentiful bandwidth, like the days of cheap and plentiful oil, may be drawing to an end. Our reliance on the network to support our businesses, our social lives and the wider economy means we may have to accept that the current price of a high-speed Internet connection is too low, and that a market correction is due.

A correction could come through differential service provision. At present, ISPs charge customers according to the speed of their connection and not by the amount of data sent and received. In the United States, network providers want to charge heavy users like YouTube and Google Videos for delivering their content. Google and other providers argue that the network should not discriminate in this way and that "network neutrality [net neutrality]" must be preserved and the current model maintained.

The days of cheap and plentiful bandwidth, like the days of cheap and plentiful oil, may be drawing to an end.

Network neutrality sounds desirable, but it creates major difficulties for providers trying to service home user demands for streamed video and still offer reliable service to businesses.

Some businesses are willing to abandon neutrality and pay more for a better service, including Alex van Someren at nCipher. "With the consumption of IP bandwidth rising fast, commercial traffic and private traffic are almost certainly going to have to be separately managed to maintain service levels. I would be happy to pay for this kind of service distinction," he says. Other companies may be less receptive. But they may have no choice if they want an Internet connection they can rely on.

Sweden Should Legalize Online File Sharing

Karl Sigfrid

In the following viewpoint, Karl Sigfrid suggests that file sharing is an inevitable technological advancement that cannot be stopped by legislation or enforcement. Any attempt to force Internet service providers to monitor file sharing and cut off users who do so is an unacceptable violation of citizens' rights. Copyrights, according to Sigfrid, are a monopoly designed to protect entertainment producers. This is an unacceptable business model, Sigfrid suggests, and he cites well-known economists who back this notion. Such copyright laws are outmoded, Sigfrid continues, and the music and film industries need to find business models that work in a technologically advanced society.

Sigfrid wrote this letter while a member of the Swedish parliament representing the Moderate Party.

As you read, consider the following questions:

1. According to Karl Sigfrid, what is the responsibility of the Internet service provider?
2. To what does the author compare the impracticality of making Internet service providers monitor their customers' online downloads?
3. What does the viewpoint suggest will inevitably happen to CDs and DVDs?

Karl Sigfrid, "Letter to the EU Commission," Sigfrid in English, February 29, 2008. Reproduced by permission of the author.

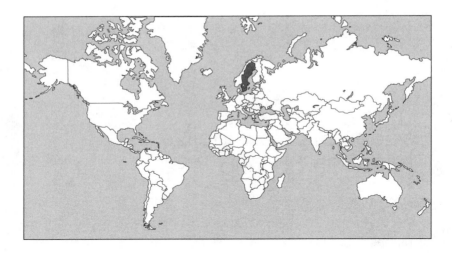

As a member of the Swedish parliament and as a Swedish citizen subjected to European Union [EU] regulation I appreciate the opportunity to give my view on the issues of file sharing and copyright law. . . .

The French Model Should Not Be Exported

The core of the French model of combating copyright violations, as described in the [European] Commission's communication, is to identify file sharers and to cut their Internet access. The ISPs [Internet service providers] then have a responsibility for the content that their subscribers download, and to enforce copyright violations some surveillance will be necessary.

In Sweden, a similar proposal has been put forward as a part of "the Renfors report [government report on how to stop the sharing]." When the Swedish government sent the Renfors proposal out to agencies and organizations for consideration, the criticism was harsh. The Swedish Court of Appeal questions whether banning citizens from the Internet would indeed reduce online file sharing. Despite several other countries having already taken similar action, none has had good results to show for it. In Finland, that has implemented this model, file-sharing activity initially dropped. However, after only three months the illegal file-sharing activities were back at previous levels.

The Swedish Data Inspection Board, responsible for safeguarding the individual's integrity, asks whether the Renfors proposal is consistent with the protection of private correspondence that is granted by the European Convention on Human Rights. EU directives as well as national legislation say that the responsibility of the Internet service providers is to offer a tool for communication—not to keep track of what individuals discuss or what information they exchange. The [Swedish] Competition Authority adds that it's unreasonable to give private businesses responsibilities that should belong to a government agency.

In Finland, that has implemented this [regulation] model, file-sharing activity initially dropped. However, after only three months the illegal file-sharing activities were back at previous levels.

Copyright Enforcement Threatens Integrity

Sweden is one of the world's most prominent technology nations, and our technology friendliness is reflected in the public opinion that views file sharing primarily as a positive phenomenon. A big part of the Swedish population favors decriminalizing all noncommercial file sharing. With our technological development, this is the only solution, unless we want an ever more extensive control of what citizens do on the Internet.

Already there are anonymization services on the market that make the currently discussed models ineffective. Putting an end to copyright infringing file sharing will demand other tools that further intensify the surveillance of the Internet.

The simple truth is that almost all communication channels on the Internet can be used to distribute copyrighted information. If you can use a service to send a message you can most likely use the same service to send an MP3 song. Those who want to prevent people from exchanging of copyrighted material must filter all electronic communication between citizens. This would be an unacceptable violation of citizens' right to privacy.

Sweden is one of the world's most prominent technology nations, and our technology friendliness is reflected in the public opinion that views file sharing primarily as a positive phenomenon.

The media industry needs reasonable rules to play by. The right to reasonable rules should apply also to Internet service providers, who don't want to be an online police force. Making broadband suppliers watch what their customers download on the Internet would be like making postal services open every package. Those who defend creators' rights should also defend everyone's right to communicate without surveillance.

Reform Protectionist Copyright Laws

There will always be industries that call for harsher legislation when the market changes. Their interest in stopping progress must be weighed against the public's interest in taking advantage of the opportunities that technology gives them. If politicians had met the demands from the copyright industry throughout history we would have had a considerably poorer media landscape; without music radio, VCRs [videocassette recorders], MP3 players. All these innovations have met political and legal resistance.

CDs and DVDs that you buy in a store or order by mail will be phased out by modern file-sharing technologies. If this

Don't Feel Sorry for Corporate Victims of Piracy

While the studios shout that piracy hurts the artists and the filmmakers and musicians, most savvies know that—AT MOST—10% of the cover price of any DVD or album will go to the original artists or production company. In many cases it's much less. When you bring creative accounting in, sometimes the people who made the project such a success will never see anything. *Forrest Gump* earned over $677 million at the box office worldwide, yet famously never made a 'profit'. *The Blair Witch Project*, the low-budget $35,000 guerilla filmmaking legend (the most profitable film ever made according to Guinness [World Records]), grossed well over $248 million at the box office alone yet the filmmakers are apparently still yet to see more than their original $1m advance. As [American actor] Richard Dreyfuss recently said, "So the guys who started this business all cheated somebody to get there, and now they're being cheated, perhaps, by all these crazy, geeky people all over the Internet. I must say, my anguish level is not great."

Nicol Wistreich, "Torrents, Piracy and Beyond:
Will the Film Industry Survive?" Netribution.co.uk,
September 4, 2006.

means the end of the recording industry as we know it, this is nothing that we can or should prevent. Attempting to stop file sharing to save the recording industry would be like outlawing cars to increase the sales of horse carriages.

While entertainment producers with old business models struggle, new businesses rise as a result of the technological shift. YouTube and Yahoo LAUNCHcast are only two out of innumerable examples of how the Internet can bring both value to consumers and revenue to producers. In fact, we should demand that everyone seeking to make a profit from selling entertainment adapts to this new reality. That means they need to have business models that are consistent with the freedom to share material on the Internet. Copyright laws, as they are designed in most Western countries, set out to protect entertainment producers by granting them a monopoly on copying and distributing their goods. Generally, we demand that entrepreneurs have business models that work without legislated monopolies. Why should this not apply to creative artists?

Generally, we demand that entrepreneurs have business models that work without legislated monopolies. Why should this not apply to creative artists?

Copyright should not be considered a property right. In *The Fatal Conceit: The Errors of Socialism*, the economist and Nobel Prize recipient F.A. [Friedrich August von] Hayek explains the difference between conventional property rights and copyright. While the supply of material resources is limited by nature, the supply of an immaterial good [is] unlimited, unless the government limits the supply by law. According to Hayek, there is no empirical evidence that copyright laws stimulate innovation. A later Nobel Prize recipient, [American economist] Milton Friedman, describes copyright as a monopoly that decreases supply to a level below the optimal level. Copyright and the regulations that follow from it should, according to Friedman, be described primarily as a limitation of free speech.

There is obviously no clear-cut, time-resistant frame defining what the government should protect as property. Neither is there empirical evidence that copyright laws need to be preserved in their current form. Therefore, I strongly react against the suggested efforts to raise "awareness on the importance of copyright for the availability of content." Such effort could not be described as education, if education is defined as spreading information based on science.

Germany Must Balance Internet Regulation with Freedom of Speech

Giampiero Giacomello

In the viewpoint that follows, Giampiero Giacomello looks at the thriving Internet culture in Germany, which ranks highly in all studies of Internet usage among countries of the world. Yet German government officials struggle with balancing freedom of speech on the Web with individual privacy. In particular, according to Giacomello, the government is highly sensitive toward neo-Nazi sites and purveyors of child pornography. Their dilemma concerns how much regulation they should enact to guard against inappropriate material, he states.

Giacomello has been a postdoctoral associate at Cornell University and a visiting professor of international relations in the Department of Politics at the University of Bologna in Italy. His research interests include international relations and security, computer networks, and cyberterrorism.

As you read, consider the following questions:

1. According to the viewpoint, what are two examples of Germans reaching consensus on Internet issues?

2. How, according to Giacomello, does German society's guilt over the Holocaust affect its attitude toward regulation of offensive Web sites?

3. How did the September 11, 2001, attacks in the United States affect attitudes toward regulation in Germany?

"Ist Deutschland fit für die digitale Ära?" the German magazine *Der Spiegel* inquired in March 2000. To external observers it indeed appeared that Germans had literally "fallen in love" with *das Netz* ("the Net"). With the exception of the Scandinavians (who are in a league of their own), Germans have been among the most active surfers on the Web, possibly preferring contents in the German language. Germany is unmistakably in the group of the world's technological "leaders." In 2000, T-Online, the Internet access provider owned by telecom giant Deutsche Telekom AG (DTAG), was the world's second-largest ISP [Internet service provider] and the most visited site of the home market. In 2001, DTAG itself entered the American mobile market and was named "Europe's biggest telecom company" by CNN. In 2002, Germany ranked number 18, after Switzerland, in the Network Readiness Index (out of 75 countries) and number 11 (out of 72) in the Technology Advancement Index of the UNDP [United Nations Development Programme] Human Development Report of 2001, just next to Singapore and before Norway. In 2003, the top-level domain for Germany (dot.ude) was the fourth most frequent country domain on the Web, and the International Telecommunication Union placed Germany in the group of countries with the highest Digital Access Index.

A Conscious Effort

These notable results are the consequence of an impressive, conscious digitalization effort by the whole of German society and economy, planned and executed through a coordinated action by the government, private industry, schools, and the media. It is the traditional logic of German orchestration and consensus among social and economic actors, with a whole new goal, namely bringing Germany into the information age and the new economy. Crucial to this endeavor is not only the full backing of the SPD-Green cabinet [a political coalition], but even the enthusiasm of Germany's industrial colossi. In Germany's corporatist democracy model, institutional actors (i.e., trade unions, industrialists' associations, consumers' groups) have fairly good access to federal and local governments and legislatures. Once consensus is reached among all these players, it endures, and the resulting policies are highly likely to be implemented. Two examples of this condition are Initiative D21 and the ICANN [Internet Corporation for Assigned Names and Numbers] at-large membership. The former case is a coherent project of the federal government and the private sector to boost IT [information technology] education in schools and society in general. In the latter case, mainly thanks to the publicity given to the event by *Spiegel Online*, a considerable number of Germans registered for the election of the new board of directors of ICANN, the organization that is responsible for domain names.

Governments Should Regulate the Internet

Shouldn't the government . . . have advanced tools to rein in online content and communications that can cause social or political strife, or disseminate illegal content or facilitate unlawful transactions? I believe it should. But the government should have some safeguards to prevent potential abuse by the regulatory and investigative bodies, too.

One way of doing this would be to pass a law to regulate the process, and to practice transparency. If it is carried out in the right manner, I think most netizens [Internet users] would not feel that their privacy is being compromised.

Victor Paul Borg,
"Filter for the Net Should Not Be a Strain,"
China Daily, July 10, 2007.

[Political scientist Arend d'Angremond] Lijphart ranks Germany mildly low in his index of pluralism. Although contemporary Germany is no longer a corporatist country as it was until the 1990s, Germany's domestic interest configuration still shows a tight coordination among interest groups. During the Cold War and the reconstruction of Germany, the federal government (Bundesregierung), the private sector, and strong trade unions cooperated tightly to produce a stable and robust economy. National security was strictly a matter for NATO [North Atlantic Treaty Organization]. After 1989, cooperation between the three players (the government, business, and trade unions) deteriorated. The government is wary about letting the private sector into national security, although it is also perfectly aware that, when it comes to Germany's NII [national information infrastructure], like all other advanced countries, there is no other alternative. Controlling the Internet for the federal government is mostly protecting the NII, with a few considerable exceptions in monitoring content. Internet stakeholders (the government, the ICT [information and communications technology] sector, and civil liberties NGOs [nongovernmental organizations]), however, still debate the typology and dimension of cyberthreats. According to the Working Group on [Critical] Infrastructure Protection . . . ICT business executives preferred low government intervention in the NII and were skeptical of cyberterrorism. A simulated cyberterrorist attack in November 2001 highlighted weak points in the NII but also confirmed the skepticism. Under these circumstances, even if the Red-Green cabinet [a political coalition] had been inclined to do so, any attempts at forcing a strong securitization move would have failed.

Notable results are the consequence of an impressive, conscious digitalization effort by the whole of German society and economy, planned and executed through a coordinated action.

Government Control vs. Freedom of Speech

With the backing of at least a portion of public opinion, the government deems it necessary to prevent the diffusion of neo-Nazi propaganda, Holocaust denial, and hatred speech or child pornography on the Internet. German civil liberties NGOs have, to some extent, opposed these policies, but they too support banning child pornography. Neo-Nazi material is more controversial, however, since civil liberties activists tend to think that, albeit despicable, it too should be protected by freedom of speech. Since the collective guilt for the past is still very strongly felt in all segments of German society, resistance to these policies has also come from American NGOs, on the basis that freedom of speech also applies to hatred or Nazi material online.

September 11[, 2001, terrorist attacks on the United States] inevitably affected Germany's approach to the Internet. However, the attacks on New York and Washington[, D.C.] in 2001, and those on Madrid [Spain] trains in 2004, did not change the German view that terrorism is "a crime," not a military endeavor. It follows that cyberterrorism is also a crime and should be dealt with by law enforcement agencies. In doing so, the federal government signaled that it would hardly try to securitize the issue of Internet control and the protection of the NII. All in all, in January 2002 the German parliament, the Bundestag, passed an antiterrorism law that allowed intelligence and law enforcement officials to access digitally stored traffic records but *not* Internet data retention. German ISPs cannot retain data on what their subscribers do when they are online. After the bombing of Madrid in March 2004, European leaders agreed to look into this matter, under the existing EU privacy guidelines, but Germany and the Scandinavians remained adamant. Even before the Madrid bombings, according to Reporters Sans Frontières [Reporters Without Borders], about twenty civil liberties and privacy NGOs had condemned the tendency to increase surveillance that the Council of Europe Convention on Cybercrime (signed in November 2003 and in force in July 2004) authorized. The treaty should help advanced, industrialized countries that are highly dependent on computer networks to fight criminality as well as terrorism on the Internet.

The government deems it necessary to prevent the diffusion of neo-Nazi propaganda, Holocaust denial, and hatred speech or child pornography on the Internet.

A Difficult Challenge

Like many other democracies, Germany faces a difficult digital challenge. It wants to remain the most technologically advanced country in Europe, protect its information infrastructure, respect freedom of speech, and defend users' privacy and decency. But it also wants to show that it is not going to forget its past and that freedom of speech cannot become a justification for hatred or Nazi nostalgia, or a loophole for child pornography.

Periodical Bibliography

The following articles have been selected to supplement the diverse views presented in this chapter.

Current Digest of the Post Soviet Press	"Will Fight Against Terror Bring Internet Censorship?" 2007.
Economist	"Bitwatching; Monitoring the Internet," May 2, 2009.
Joachim Frenk	"Freedom Filtered: On Internet Censorship in the UK," *Journal for the Study of British Cultures*, February 2008.
Jackie Granick	"Iranian Internet Censorship," *Harvard International Review*, Summer 2005.
Zhanna Kozhamberdiyeva	"Freedom of Expression on the Internet: A Case Study of Uzbekistan," *Review of Central and East European Law*, 2008.
Rebecca MacKinnon	"Flatter World and Thicker Walls? Blogs, Censorship and Civic Discourse in China," *Public Choice*, January 2008.
Maclean's	"Yes, Master: The Recent Controversy over Internet Censorship Has Exposed a Nasty Truth About China's Economic Miracle: How Western Companies Are Selling Out Human Rights for Profits," 2006.
Matthew Quirk	"The Web Police," *Atlantic*, May 2006.
Brian Simpson	"New Labor, New Censorship? Politics, Religion and Internet Filtering in Australia," *Information & Communications Technology Law*, October 2008.
Lokman Tsui	"An Inadequate Metaphor: The Great Firewall and Chinese Internet Censorship," *Global Dialogue*, Winter/Spring 2007.

GLOBALVIEWPOINTS

CHAPTER 4

Cybercrime
and Cyberwar

Nigeria Must Crack Down on Its Cybercriminals

Zakariyya Adaramola

In the following viewpoint, Zakariyya Adaramola writes that Nigeria has been slow to fight the spread of cybercrime in its own country. Uneducated Nigerian consumers are particularly susceptible to the wiles of Internet con men, who are preying on an increasing number of people using more and more sophisticated means. Mallan Nuhu Ribadu, who formerly oversaw the fight against cybercrime in Nigeria, was fairly successful in his job, but since his departure, cybercriminals have resumed their activities with increasing frequency. Unless Nigeria is vigilant against such criminals, Internet fraud and other cybercrimes will continue unabated.

Adaramola is a Nigerian who writes for IT World *and* Daily Trust.

As you read, consider the following questions:

1. According to the article, despite the abuses perpetrated by Mallam Nuhu Ribadu while in office, how did he successfully fight cybercrime?
2. According to Solomon Edun, where does Nigeria rank among the top 10 countries susceptible to Internet fraud?

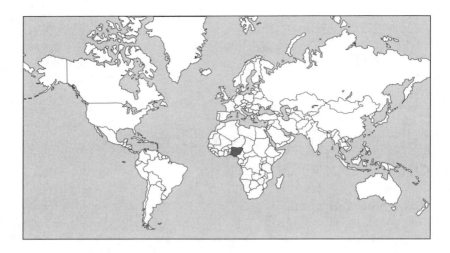

3. How has InterSwitch attempted to educate its cardholders about the dangers of fraud, according to its managing director?

Internet-based attacks and crimes are increasing in Nigeria as "greedy" criminals continue to steal data from businesses and individuals.

The sad story however is [the Nigerian] government's attitude to curb the menace. *IT World's* Zakariyya Adaramola, wrote on the implications of the delay to act fast on the criminals.

Mallam Nuhu Ribadu, the former chairman of the Economic and Financial Crimes Commission (EFCC), may have been used by the immediate former president, Chief Olusegun Obasanjo, to harass and intimidate those perceived as enemies of his government, especially those who fought against the third term agenda, but the anti-financial crime agency under Ribadu did something very well: the fight to reduce cyber-related crimes in the country. Under Ribadu, the EFCC put many measures on ground to curtail cybercrimes and a number of arrests of the so-called Yahoo Boys.

New Dangers from Cybercrime Attacks

But no sooner was Ribadu booted out of [the] EFCC that the "profit-driven" cybercriminals resumed and even increased and perfected their activities. They are daily becoming sophisticated so much so that cyberexperts are warning that if government fails to do something to stop them, many Nigerians may be in danger of fresh attacks. This is because cybercriminals, experts said, are now discovering new ways to exploit people, networks and the Internet and many people are very vulnerable to such attacks.

The managing director of Global InfoSwift, a Lagos-based IT [information technology] firm, Mr. Solomon Edun, said theft and other fraudulent practices being committed online are increasing by the day and many are being stolen by the day.

> *Cybercriminals . . . are now discovering new ways to exploit people, networks and the Internet and many people are very vulnerable to such attacks.*

According to Mr. Edun, Nigeria is the third among the top 10 countries which are highly susceptible to fraudulent attacks through electronic mails and Web pages. He said the statistics from Internet Crime Complaint Center highlights an ever-increasing concern around the nature and dynamics [of] the fraudulent attacks . . . taking place.

He said the financial services continue to be the most targeted sector at 91.7% of all attacks recorded in December 2007 only, adding that this trend is there to continue if necessary steps are not urgently taken.

His words: "According to 2007 Internet Crime Report, Internet crime resulted in nearly $240 million in reported losses in 2007, a $40 million increase over reported losses in 2006.

"As financial institutions in Nigeria are merging complex IT infrastructures and merging their products and services online, their vulnerability and intellectual property theft is increasing.

"The retrieval of consumers' personal identity data and financial account credentials is often achieved by stealing credentials directly using key-logging mechanisms and phisher-controlled proxies or by misdirecting users to non-authentic Web sites."

"The goal of awareness campaign is crucial to increase the level of security awareness of the banking customers and encourage electronic interactions amongst the banks in Nigeria," he said.

Some Nigerians are . . . victims of criminals who daily send scam mails to e-mail addresses, telling them to register their ATM cards.

Internet Cons Gain Private Information

As did Edun, a world-renowned IT company, Cisco [Systems], also warned that fraudsters would wreak more havoc online this year than they did last year [2008] and 2007 put together. In the 2008 edition of the Cisco Annual Security Report made available to *Daily Trust* in Lagos, the company said more businesses and individuals may have their data stolen, adding that fraudsters may also gain access to accounts of cardholders. And this has been happening as some Nigerians are fallen victims of criminals who daily send scam mails to e-mail addresses, telling them to register their ATM [automated teller machine] cards.

These mails, purportedly from InterSwitch [an electronic transaction company], request ATM cardholders to confirm their cards because "our services are being upgraded to a new better and more secured system." The fraudsters even threaten

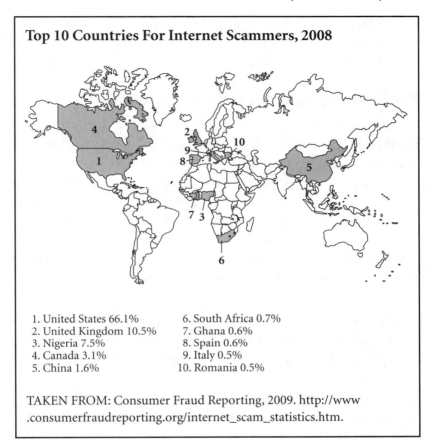

Top 10 Countries For Internet Scammers, 2008

1. United States 66.1%
2. United Kingdom 10.5%
3. Nigeria 7.5%
4. Canada 3.1%
5. China 1.6%
6. South Africa 0.7%
7. Ghana 0.6%
8. Spain 0.6%
9. Italy 0.5%
10. Romania 0.5%

TAKEN FROM: Consumer Fraud Reporting, 2009. http://www
.consumerfraudreporting.org/internet_scam_statistics.htm.

that anyone who fails to register his/her card "immediately will no longer be able to use the card with ATM machines or ATM transactions and the card will be cancelled or terminated."

But InterSwitch Limited has dissociated itself from mails being sent to mailboxes requesting ATM cardholders to register their cards, saying the mails did not emanate from the company. Speaking with *Daily Trust*, the managing director [MD] of InterSwitch, Mr. Mitchell Elegbe, swiftly dissociated the company from such mails, saying fraudsters are at work and that cardholders should be ware. According to Mr. Elegbe, InterSwitch would never tell any of its cardholders to reveal their PINs [personal identification numbers] under any guise. He said this is not the first time the mails of this type are being circulated, warning Nigerians not to fall prey of fraudsters.

Public Awareness Must Be Intensified

The InterSwitch MD said the company would intensify the cardholders' awareness campaign began last year. He explained that the main objective of the campaign, which is already running on radio, newspapers, magazines and billboards, is to protect cardholders from fraudsters, who tamper with ATM cards' PINs in order to have access to cardholders' bank accounts. According to Mr. Elegbe, the campaign is being sponsored jointly by InterSwitch and banks, and would continue to run until all cardholders are fully aware of fraudsters.

> *The rapid growth in card adoption and usage only goes to indicate the potential of well-orchestrated nefarious activities targeted at not only the unsuspecting cardholders but also the banks.*

"With the introduction of payment cards in the country, adoption of all forms [of] electronic payment channels ranging from automated teller machines (ATMs), point of sales (POS) terminals, kiosk, voice, Internet banking and mobile banking have been on a steady rise.

"The rapid growth in card adoption and usage only goes to indicate the potential of well-orchestrated nefarious activities targeted at not only the unsuspecting cardholders but also the banks. Whilst instances where cardholders have fallen victim to these activities represent far less than 1% of all transactions, they have raised fears amongst current and potential cardholders as to the security of the cardholder and payment done using cards. And that is why we have begun a cardholders awareness campaign to protect them from fraudsters", said the InterSwitch boss.

Though the Anti Money Laundering and Cyber Crime Coalition at the National Assembly last met with some EFCC officials, bank officials and some computer professionals on the need to intensify the fight against cybercrimes and money laundering in the country, not much was heard after that.

The Need for New Legislation

To effectively tackle the problem of economic and widespread Internet fraud in the country, experts said, there must be enabling legislation, as the absence of enabling legislation to properly spell out punishment for offenders has been responsible for the increasing rate of cybercrimes in the country. And until government does that, cybercrimes will continue to increase in the country.

VIEWPOINT 2

Russian Organized Crime Pervades the World Wide Web

Rob Sharp

According to Rob Sharp in the following viewpoint, Russian organized crime has its tentacles all over the world via the Internet. After briefly disappearing from view, this shadowy organization, the Russian Business Network (RBN) has evolved and reappeared by moving its base of operations to China. The RBN engages in a host of illegal operations, Sharp claims, including "phishing," pornography, identity theft, and corporate blackmail. Similar organizations, such as the ShadowCrew, have also been prominent players in illegal Internet activity. Despite the best efforts of government authorities to shut down such organizations, cybercrime worldwide is booming, in the author's view.

Sharp writes for Ireland's Belfast Telegraph.

As you read, consider the following questions:

1. According to the viewpoint, who is thought to be the mastermind behind the Russian Business Network?

2. How does Sharp claim the Russian Business Network communicates with its potential users?

3. Why has the Russian Business Network moved its base of operations to China, in the author's view?

Rob Sharp, "Cybercrime: Uncovered," *Belfast Telegraph* (Ireland), February 13, 2008. Copyright © belfasttelegraph.co.uk. Reproduced by permission. www.independent .co.uk.

192

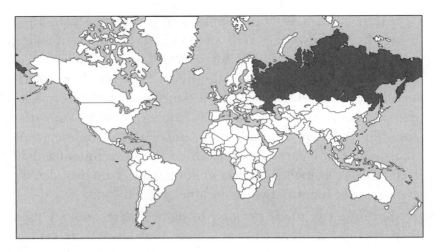

The criminal mastermind lives somewhere in Russia. Drawing on his links to the underworld, he uses the Internet to pull the strings of a shadowy network of misanthropes allegedly connected to the Kremlin [Russian government].

Nothing escapes this kingpin's malevolence: online pornography, fraud, corporate blackmail—it all causes his coffers to fill and his ego to grow. And therein lies his problem. He gets cocky. Known only as "Flyman", his notoriety spreads and the attention forces him to go to ground.

The Explosion of Web-Based Crime

It sounds like a piece of [American mystery novelist] Raymond Chandler for the noughties [the first decade of the 2000s], a hybrid of films like *Hackers*, *The Matrix* or any cyberpunk thriller from the past 20 years. But it is, in fact, real. The network is the Russian Business Network (RBN)— thought to be led by the nephew of a well-connected Russian politician—and it has been attracting the attention of security experts worldwide. Now, after briefly disappearing off the radar, it is believed that the group has moved its operations to China.

Meanwhile, in Britain, members of a similar organisation using the ShadowCrew Web site could face stiff sentencing next month [March 2008] for online fraud. Wherever you look, Web-based crime is in the news. Everyone has experienced the annoyance of an e-mail claiming to come from a legitimate bank, asking for account details (a process known as "phishing"). There are millions of incidences of online crime in Britain each year. At a time when the government is still reeling from losing 25 million child benefit claimants' details, concern over identity theft is in a heightened state.

But online crime is not easy to fight. The technology used to perpetrate it often runs at a pace that lawmakers cannot match. And having your bank account drained by a fraudster in China is akin to being pickpocketed from halfway around the world.

Wherever you look, Web-based crime is in the news.

The Russian Business Network Evolves

Take the RBN. It is thought to be behind as much as half of every incident of "phishing" worldwide. It first came to the attention of security experts 18 months ago. Acting as an Internet service provider, it soon began allowing criminals to host illegal Web sites, arguing that its own activities were not illegal; it was just the people using its services that were breaking the law.

The organisation does not communicate with its potential users through conventional means. Instead, it posts advertisements on underground bulletin boards. According to SecureWorks, an Atlanta-based security company, those who want to buy its services can also contact its operators through instant-messaging services. Potential customers also must prove they are not law enforcement officers, sometimes by proving they were involved in criminal activity.

Vitaliy Kamlyuk, a virus analyst at Russian computer security firm Kaspersky [Lab], has been following RBN's activities. Since October [2007], something strange has been happening: One by one, the Web sites linked to the organisation have closed down. But its *modus operandi* has been spotted across the Far East. RBN is not shutting down, it's diversifying. "We suppose that the organisation has been planning this for a long time," Kamlyuk says, "but the attention it has gained has speeded up its activity. We believe they had connections with Chinese servers; and criminals trying to hide often go to Malaysia, China, Korea or Japan."

It is thought the organisation is using China because the country's huge number of Internet users makes the group's activities hard to monitor. There has been talk in Russia about introducing a clampdown on Internet crime, and service providers around the world have blocked many of RBN's Web sites.

RBN [the Russian Business Network, a cybercrime ring] is not shutting down, it's diversifying.

Keeping Pace and Fighting Cybercrime

The race is on to spot the RBN's new Web sites. Raimund Genes, the chief technology officer of Trend Micro, one of the big US-based Internet security firms, says he has linked the organisation to attacks on the Turkish and Brazilian governments. "What has happened at RBN has been related to all kinds of attacks on the Internet," he says. "I believe they have been too greedy."

Genes has found that the RBN has been behind the registration of scores of Web sites in China—and says the Chinese authorities are aware of this. Whether RBN plans to sell these sites on or run them itself, only time will tell. He has also spotted the RBN's techniques at work in Panama.

Genes concludes: "We can't believe there is so much criminal activity out there. Previously infections and viruses used to be spread by e-mail attachments. Now the big thing is spreading by visits to Web pages."

In Britain, the Serious Organised Crime Agency is hoping for a strict sentence for members of a crime ring that used ShadowCrew, an American Web site that shared the know-how needed to set up phishing rackets. The Web site was investigated by US authorities in October 2004 and a spate of arrests followed.

The crime ring using the ShadowCrew Web site was organised by Bryn Wellman, 35, who was sentenced to 10 years in prison on charges for conspiring to obtain up to £16m [sixteen million British pounds] by fraud earlier this year. Wellman's scheme involved buying stolen [credit] card details online and researching cardholders' personal information using various techniques (including impersonating officials to phone up unsuspecting victims). Other members of his crime ring face sentencing next month [March 2008].

Worldwide Cybercrime Is Booming

But whatever happens to RBN and ShadowCrew, one thing is for sure: Cybercrime is booming.

Whatever happens to RBN and ShadowCrew, one thing is for sure: Cybercrime is booming.

Israel. In the first six months of this year, Israel had the most malicious activity per Internet user. In 2005, investigators revealed that a "Trojan Horse" program had infiltrated some 60 companies, which became Israel's biggest corporate espionage scandal. A swathe of companies came under investigation for allegedly stealing information from rivals.

United States. Online fraud has overtaken viruses as the greatest source of financial loss in the US. According to

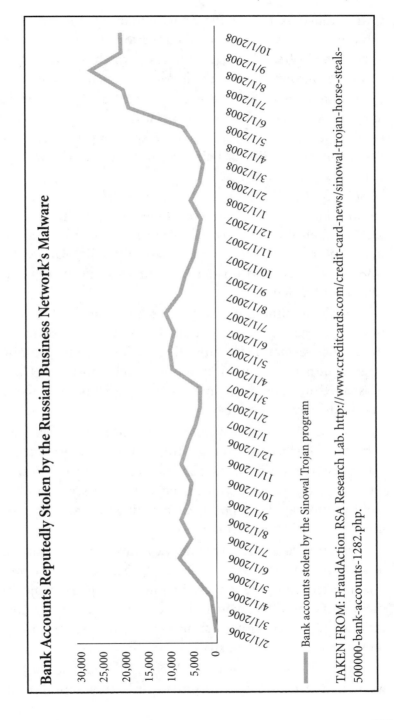

Bank Accounts Reputedly Stolen by the Russian Business Network's Malware

—— Bank accounts stolen by the Sinowal Trojan program

TAKEN FROM: FraudAction RSA Research Lab. http://www.creditcards.com/credit-card-news/sinowal-trojan-horse-steals-500000-bank-accounts-1282.php.

California-based security firm Symantec, in the first six months of this year the US accounted for 61 per cent of world-wide denial-of-service (DoS) attacks, which attempt to make computer resources unavailable to their intended users.

Panama. In these countries—as well as Turkey, Malaysia and Singapore—the Russian Business Network is alleged to operate servers. The locations are disparate presumably in order to spread the risk of being permanently shut down by one country's police force.

United Kingdom. Around 3 million Internet crimes were committed in the UK last year. One of the most common is identity theft. In 2004, two people were arrested over an Internet crime ring, the ShadowCrew, that allegedly planned to defraud consumers and financial institutions out of hundreds of millions of dollars.

Nigeria. Online fraud is a burgeoning business in this nation. One trick is to lure potential victims into a scam via an unsolicited e-mail. The unwitting recipients are promised a large commission on a multibillion-dollar fortune. They are persuaded to open an online account, to which they contribute funds, never to be seen again.

Russia. The shadowy Russian Business Network was reportedly launched by young computer science graduates and was registered as an Internet site last year. After a period of legitimate activity, it has since been linked by security firms to child pornography, corporate blackmail, spam attacks and online identity theft across the globe.

China. Bots are software applications that run automated tasks over the Internet. China has 29 per cent of the world's bot-infected computers, with Beijing hosting the majority of these. Bots are often benign, but can be used for various nefarious tasks, such as harvesting e-mail addresses from address books to help distribute spam.

Estonia. Last year, Russian Web users launched a "cyberwar" on the Estonian government, infecting 1 million computers with "bots". This overwhelmed the country's networks by requesting more information than they were designed to cope with. The effect was equivalent to 5,000 clicks per second and many Web sites were forced to shut down.

Canada. In 2004, US Secret Service agents arrested members of the ShadowCrew in Canada, who were using the Web site to orchestrate document forgery and drug operations. In Vancouver, one of their number was just 17; he saw online underworld activities as a "rebellion against authority" according to reports.

Terrorist Organizations Use the Internet for Recruitment

Gabriel Weimann

In this viewpoint, Gabriel Weimann warns about the new Internet tactics being used by al Qaeda and other terrorist organizations to attract women and children to their causes. Specifically, terrorist organizations are using the market technique of "narrowcasting," that is, targeting specific age or gender groups by appealing narrowly to their interests. Terrorist organizations particularly want to recruit women and children to become suicide bombers, or, failing that extreme, to at least support those who do engage in violent jihad. Terrorists organizations are now using sophisticated marketing appeals, says Weimann, and their success is evident in the increasing number of those involved in suicide terrorism.

Weimann is a professor of communications at the University of Haifa in Israel. He has written widely on modern terrorism, political campaigns, and the mass media. He is the author of Terror on the Internet: The New Arena, the New Challenges.

As you read, consider the following questions:

1. According to Weimann, how many Web sites does al Qaeda operate?

2. How does al Qaeda encourage women to join in terrorist operations, in the author's view?

3. According to the viewpoint, what kind of advice does the online magazine *Al-Khansaa* offer for women?

As the Internet matures so has the terrorist use of this ideal instrument of communication. Following the path of modern Western advertising techniques, terrorist organizations have begun "narrowcasting," or making targeted pitches for recruitment and support among specific demographics like women and children.

The Internet has long been a favorite tool of the terrorists. Decentralized and providing almost perfect anonymity, it cannot be subjected to control or restriction, and allows access to anyone who wants it. Large or small, terrorist groups have their own Web sites, using this medium to spread propaganda, raise funds and launder money, recruit and train members, communicate and conspire, plan and launch attacks. Al Qaeda, for example, now operates approximately 5,600 Web sites, and 900 more appear each year. Besides Web sites, modern terrorists rely on e-mail, chat rooms, e-groups, forums, virtual message boards, and resources like YouTube and Google Earth.

Terrorists recognize the Internet's popularity among children and youth. One of Hamas's Web sites, Al-Fateh, or "The Conqueror," appears every other week and is designed for children, with cartoon-style designs and colorful children's stories. The site's title promises "pages discussing jihad, scientific pages, the best stories, not be found elsewhere, and unequalled tales of heroism." The Al-Fateh site has a link to the official Hamas site, www.palestine-info.com.

Mixed among children's songs and stories written by children themselves are messages promoting suicide terrorism. Thus, the site presented the gruesome photo of a decapitated head of young Zainab Abu Salem, a female suicide bomber who on September 22, 2004, detonated an explosive belt in Jerusalem, killing two policemen and wounding 17 civilians. The caption praises the act, arguing that she is now in paradise, a "shaheeda" like her male comrades: "Her head was severed from her pure body and her headscarf remained to decorate [her face]. Your place is in heaven in the upper skies, oh, Zainab, sister [raised to the status of heroic] men."

The same website posted the last will of a Hamas suicide bomber, who, on June 1, 2001, carried out a suicide bombing attack at the Dolphinarium, a Tel Aviv teen club. The attack resulted in the deaths of 21 Israeli civilians, most of them teenagers. In his online will, the suicide bomber writes: "I will turn my body into shrapnel and bombs, which will chase the children of Zion, will blow them up and will burn what is left of them. . . . There is nothing greater than killing oneself on the land of Palestine, for the sake of Allah."

Mixed among children's songs and stories written by children themselves are messages promoting suicide terrorism.

Computer games are another online tactic targeting youth. Several terrorist groups offer free online games, designed as instruments of radicalization and training. One such game is the *Quest for Bush*, aka *Night of Bush Capturing*, a free online game released by the Global Islamic Media Front, a media outlet of al Qaeda. Armed with a rifle, a shotgun or a grenade launcher, players navigate missions that include "Jihad Growing Up," "Americans' Hell" and "Bush Hunted Like a Rat." In the final stage, the player's task is to kill President Bush.

Another example is Hezbollah's *Special Force*, an online game that allows players to become warriors in a terrorist campaign against Israel. The violent game features a training mode in which participants practice shooting skills on former Israeli Prime Minister Ariel Sharon and other Israeli figures. A "high score" earns a certificate signed by Hezbollah leader

Nasrallah and presented in a "cyberceremony." At the end of the game the players receive a display of Hezbollah "martyrs"—fighters killed by Israel.

Several terrorist groups offer free online games, designed as instruments of radicalization and training.

In August 2007, a new version emerged, entitled *Special Force 2*. Based on the 2006 Lebanon War between Hezbollah and Israel, the game was produced by Hezbollah. Available in Arabic, English, French and Farsi, the game allows players to take on the role of a Hezbollah combatant in a 3D environment.

A number of Islamist Web sites include forums for women. Examples include www.al-hesbah.org/v, www.shmo5alislam.net and www.al-faloja.info/vb. The objective of these forums is essentially indoctrination. They encourage women to carry out suicide attacks, for example, by posting biographies and testaments of female martyrs from Islamic history and modern times. They also promote jihad by citing various Fatwas on jihad and martyrdom, urging women to take an active role or at least support its fighters.

In Al-Hesbah forum, a writer called Umm Hamza Al-Shahid posted a July 2007 message titled "Secure Yourself a Chandelier Under the Throne [in Paradise]," encouraging Muslim women to carry out suicide bombings. The posting includes this call: "Sister, do you fear the horror of death and the agony of dying? Don't you wish for such an end—an easy transition from this world to Paradise, without pain or agony. . . . Since death is inevitable, why should we not leave this transient [world] in our best capacity, [that is,] as martyrs?"

In the ninth issue of *Sawt al-Jihad*, or *Voice of Jihad*, al Qaeda's online magazine was the first in a series of postings targeting women, including a special section for women and attempting to recruit women for terrorist attacks.

One of the articles, "Um Hamza, an Example for the Woman Holy Warrior," tells the story of martyr, the late Um Hamza, as told by her husband: "Um Hamza was very happy whenever she heard about a martyrdom operation carried out by a woman, whether it was in Palestine or Chechnya. She used to cry because she wanted a martyrdom operation against the Christians in the Arabian Peninsula."

Later, al Qaeda launched its online women's magazine called *Al-Khansaa*, named after an early Islamic poetess who wrote eulogies for Muslims who died while fighting "infidels." The Web site gives advice on raising children to carry on the jihad, providing first aid for a family member injured in combat and physical training needed to prepare for fighting.

The magazine's goal seems to be teaching women married to Islamists how to support their husbands in their violent war against the non-Muslim world. An early article reads: "The blood of our husbands and the body parts of our children are our sacrificial offering."

Increasing participation of women and youth in suicide terrorism may serve as alarming signals of narrowcasting's success.

Likewise, a series of messages regarding the Muslim woman and her role in supporting war on the West emerged on jihadist forums. One document, titled "What Do the Mujahideen Want from a Muslim Woman?" was written by Abu Omar Abdul Bar, a leading Muslim writer, and charges that the war launched by the West against Islam is not limited to direct military action. It also seeks to affect changes in economic, social and character. In this regard, Abu Omar suggests that the enemy attempts to alienate Muslim women within their community and "spoil them."

Terrorist Web Sites Attract Middle-Class Followers

There are some general hypotheses as to why people from the seemingly secular middle class—and specifically scientists and people in technological fields—are driven to militant Islam. Islam fills a spiritual need in their lives, dominated by scientific inquiry and reason. As the Singapore white paper stated, what drove them was their religiosity: "Most detainees regarded religion as their most important personal value." Other hypotheses suggest that being computer savvy, they "learn their Islam online" and are drawn to jihadist Web sites. Some of the most technically proficient sites offer Koranic interpretations, video clips from jihads in far-flung corners of the world, and ample evidence of egregious and violent persecution of fellow Muslims. The Internet creates a virtual community for Muslims that allows alienated Muslim youth to find a "responsive and compassionate forum." As the French scholar Gilles Kepel said about the Internet, "It erases the frontiers between the *dar al-Islam* (House of Islam or Peace) and the *dar al-Kufr* (House of the Unbeliever). It allows the propagation of a universal norm, with an Internet *sharia* [Islamic law] and *fatwa* [an Islamic legal ruling] system."

James J.F. Forest, ed.
The Making of a Terrorist:
Recruitment, Training, and Root Causes, Westport, CT:
Praeger Security International, 2005.

Opposed to the Western desire to make a "cheap commodity" of women, the message advocates the role of a woman as a mujahid, citing examples of female mujahideen in Muslim history. Abu Omar writes that a Muslim woman should feed her sons "gunpowder with milk," adding "we want from her to be a factory of heroes and her house to be a lion's den."

These examples are only a few from numerous online sites, but the trend is clear: Terrorist fine-tune their appeals, sharpening their messages according to narrowly defined sub-populations. Success, according to advanced marketing theory and research, is guaranteed.

Sophisticated persuasion is more likely to succeed when the medium, stimuli, appeals and graphics are tailored to specific receivers. Increasing participation of women and youth in suicide terrorism may serve as alarming signals of narrow-casting's success.

Australia Must Fight Internet Crime and Support Its Victims

Lynne Roberts

In this viewpoint, Lynne Roberts provides examples of how Australia is fighting Internet crime and suggests that even more programs are needed to fight an ever-increasing amount of online predators. Roberts especially focuses on the individuals who are targets of Internet crime, who are rarely given the necessary help to deal with their victimization. Additionally, Roberts suggests a host of measures, from Internet filters for children to educational training, which can make Web surfers more aware of the pitfalls of Internet use. Finally, Roberts suggests that more studies are needed to deal adequately with this burgeoning type of victimization.

Roberts is a lecturer in the School of Psychology at Curtin University of Technology in Perth, Australia.

As you read, consider the following questions:

1. What group in Australia is charged with providing a national approach to Internet crime, according to Roberts?
2. As the author reports, what type of anticrime operations are Australian police using at the state level?
3. According to the viewpoint, what percentage of Australian homes use Internet filters?

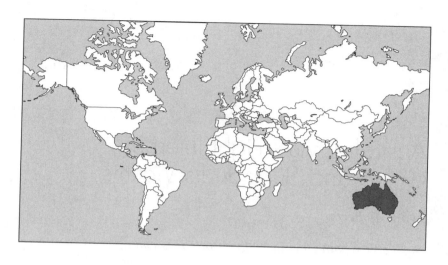

All governments have an ethical responsibility to address the needs of victims of crime, and this includes the victims of cybercrimes. While most Western countries, including Australia, offer a range of services to crime victims, only a minority of victims avail themselves of these services, tending to rely instead on the support of family and friends. Cybercrimes are relatively new crimes and responses to cyber-victimisation are still developing. These include legal, technical, regulatory, educational and professional responses.

Legal Responses Face Challenges

The justice needs of cyber-victims may be partially met through the criminal investigation of cybercrimes and prosecution of cyber-offenders. This is dependent on the existence of laws covering cybercrimes and the willingness of police to investigate cybercrimes. Some cybercrime offences are already covered under existing laws or through the introduction or amendment of legislation to cover online instances of existing criminal behaviours. However, the key issue hampering legal responses is that while cybercrime is global, most laws are restricted to nations or states and the investigation and prosecution of cybercrimes is reliant on cooperation between jurisdictions. Cooperation is currently hindered by the lack of consistent definitions of cybercrimes and inconsistencies in the sanctions imposed across jurisdictions. Within Australia, the Australian High Tech Crime Centre is charged with providing a national coordinated approach to cybercrime investigation and of improving the capacity of jurisdictions to deal with cybercrime.

[J.] Blindell reviewed the legal status and rights of identity theft victims in Australia. In most states of Australia, identity theft victims are not classified as victims of crime and are consequently not eligible for existing victims' rights and services. The report highlighted the need for the development of a specific identity theft offence and the explicit inclusion of identity theft victims within statutory definitions of victims. These statutory rights should include the recovery of costs relating to reporting the theft, preventive action to limit further use and financial reputation restoration; the right to access victim assistance services; the right to victim certificates and to have victim affidavits recognised; and the right to present victim impact statements to sentencing courts. Similarly, to effectively respond to the growing identity crime problems, identity theft needs to be made a federal crime in Australia.

To effectively respond to the growing identity crime problems, identity theft needs to be made a federal crime in Australia.

Within Australia, the Australian Federal Police established an Online Child Sexual Exploitation Team (OCSET) in January 2005, to provide a national assessment and coordination capability for international and national referrals of child pornography. In 2005/2006, OCSET made 21 arrests and secured ten convictions/guilty pleas on charges relating to the possession and transmission of child pornography and cyber-grooming.

At the state level, police 'sting' operations have been established in Western Australia and Queensland. These operations involve police officers posing as children or youth online in order to attract and identify paedophiles. The police officers do not initiate sexual discussions but respond to advances. In Queensland, the police officers pose as girls aged 13 to 16 years. The activities engaged in by 'suspects' during these stings included meeting off-line to perform a sexual act, discussing sex and sexual acts in general, discussing sexual acts involving the child, sending sexually explicit material, online masturbation using a Web cam and making offers of reward for sexual services.

Legislative and investigative approaches are unlikely to be sufficient to enable the investigation and prosecution of all cybercrimes, highlighting the need for police to establish a network of relationships in order to effectively police cybercrimes. The majority of cybercriminal activities are resolved without police involvement and working relationships need to be established between police and Internet user groups, online virtual environment managers, network infrastructure providers, corporate security organisations, and nongovernmental and governmental non-police organizations in order to effectively 'police' cyberspace.

Possible Solutions to Cybercrime

Technical solutions may be utilised to reduce or 'design out' some types of cybercrimes, typically through the filtering, blocking and monitoring of digital data. Internet filters such as 'Net Nanny' are employed to block content unsuitable for children. Approximately one in five Australian adolescents report that software filters are used at home. However, no blocking or filtering system provides complete accuracy in the material that is blocked. For example, recent Australian tests of the efficacy of server-based Internet content filters found that the best of the filters blocked only 76% of content that should

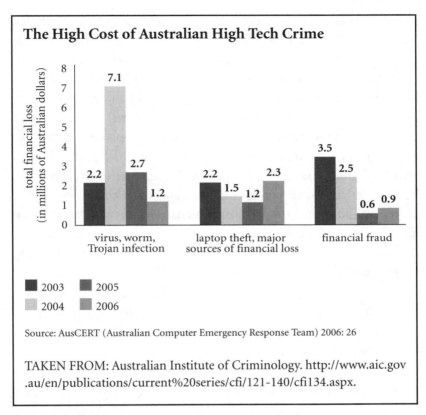

The High Cost of Australian High Tech Crime

Source: AusCERT (Australian Computer Emergency Response Team) 2006: 26

TAKEN FROM: Australian Institute of Criminology. http://www.aic.gov
.au/en/publications/current%20series/cfi/121-140/cfi134.aspx.

be blocked. Filtering and blocking systems need to be updated continuously to retain any form of currency.

Industry codes of practice and standards have been advocated as a means of controlling cybercrimes. Within Australia, the relevant government regulatory body for information and communication technologies is the Australian Communications and Media Authority (ACMA). The Internet Industry Association is currently developing the *IIA Cybercrime Code of Practice*. The degree to which the onus of detecting and reporting of cybercrimes should be the responsibility of Internet service providers is contentious.

All Internet users need to be aware of how to protect their personal information online and how to interact safely within virtual environments. Materials relating to Internet safety are readily available online. For example, NetAlert, the Web site of Australia's Internet safety advisory board, contains a wide range of information on Internet safety directed at parents, teachers, librarians and children. This includes online interactive educational games that are targeted at children of different ages. Parents, teachers and caregivers will need to keep abreast of changing technologies in order to protect children.

An Internet harassment component should be added to all anti-bullying programs in schools. Prevention efforts need to be targeted at those youth most at risk, with education about sexual solicitation targeted at preteens and teens. Reporting of all types of online harassment should be promoted, with increased options for reporting, and the reasons for reporting emphasised.

All Internet users need to be aware of how to protect their personal information online and how to interact safely within virtual environments.

Support services to cybercrime victims may be provided on or off-line, through existing agencies supporting all types of crime victims, or through specialised services. Professionals working with cybercrime victims need to be familiar with the varying impacts of cyber-victimisation and the needs of victims. Mental health professionals need to be aware of online sexual predatory behaviour in order to recognise the signs of children and youth who may be victims and to become sensitised to their needs. Cybercrime victims (children, youth and adults) may present with online victimisation as the primary presenting problem, or with a range of online and off-line problems.

A Wide-Ranging Effort Is Needed

Information and communication technologies create new opportunities for criminal activities. New forms of cybercrime will continue to emerge with the introduction of new information and communication technologies and are likely to produce new victims. Victims will vary in their responses to cybercriminal acts and not all will experience distress or require access to victims' services. Combinations of strategies will be required to effectively prevent cyber-victimisation. For example, the need for a combination of technical solutions, education, parental monitoring and legal responses have been proposed as essential to protect children from sexual exploitation online. Where prevention activities are not effective, crisis intervention, counselling, advocacy and support services will need to be equipped to deal sensitively with those cyber-victims who do require help. To inform this service provision, further research is required into the impact of cyber-victimisation and appropriate responses.

Globally, Cyberwarfare Is a Threat to National Security

Kenneth Geers

According to cyberdefense specialist Kenneth Geers, several major attacks in the 1990s and early 2000s, including those on Chechnya, Kosovo, the Middle East, the United States, China, and Estonia, ushered in an era of cyberwar. Geers argues in the following viewpoint that every conflict from this point forward will have a cyber component in which countries either use their own Internet resources for propaganda and communications or block the capabilities of others. Because cyberdefense is a relatively new concept, nations are often unprepared for the havoc caused by aggressors. National security planners must be aware of the cyber dimension to new conflicts and plan for any contingency, Geers warns.

Geers is the U.S. representative of the Naval Criminal Investigative Service to the Cooperative Cyber Defence Centre of Excellence, based in Tallinn, Estonia.

As you read, consider the following questions:

1. According to Geers, why is cyberdefense still an immature discipline?
2. What conflict does Geers believe was the first broadscale Internet war?
3. Which Israeli business Web sites were attacked by pro-Palestinian hackers in 2006?

Kenneth Geers, "Cyberspace and the Changing Nature of Warfare" *SC Magazine*, August 27, 2008. Copyright © 2008 Haymarket Media, Inc. Reproduced by permission.

Practically everything that happens in the real world is mirrored in cyberspace.

For national security planners, this includes propaganda, espionage, reconnaissance, targeting, and—to a limited extent—warfare itself.

Strategists must be aware that part of every political and military conflict will take place on the Internet, whose ubiquitous and unpredictable characteristics mean that the battles fought there can be just as important, if not more so, than events taking place on the ground.

Aggressive cyberwarfare strategies and tactics offer many advantages to their prospective employers, and current events demonstrate that cyberconflict is already commonplace around the world. As a consequence, national security leadership must dramatically improve its understanding of the technology, law, and ethics of cyber attack and defense, so that it can competently factor cyberwarfare into all stages of national security planning.

Part of every political and military conflict will take place on the Internet, whose ubiquitous and unpredictable characteristics mean that the battles fought there can be just as important [as] events taking place on the ground.

Cyberwarfare Is an Ideal Strategy

The Internet's imperfect design allows hackers to surreptitiously read, delete, and/or modify information stored on or traveling between computers. There are about 100 additions to the Common Vulnerabilities and Exposures (CVE) database each month. Attackers, armed with constantly evolving malicious code, likely have more paths into your network and the secrets it contains than your system administrators can protect.

The objectives of cyberwarfare practitioners speak for themselves: the theft of research and development data, eavesdropping on sensitive communications, and the delivery of powerful propaganda deep behind enemy lines (to name a few). The elegance of computer hacking lies in the fact that it may be attempted for a fraction of the cost—and risk—of any other information collection or manipulation strategy.

Cyberdefense is still an immature discipline. Traditional law enforcement skills are inadequate, and it is difficult to retain personnel with highly marketable technical skills. Challenging computer investigations are further complicated by the international nature of the Internet. Finally, in the case of state-sponsored computer network operations, law enforcement cooperation will be either Potemkin [misleading] or nonexistent.

The maze-like architecture of the Internet offers cyberattackers a high degree of anonymity. Smart hackers can route attacks through countries with which the victim's government has poor diplomatic relations and no law enforcement cooperation. Even successful investigations often lead only to another hacked computer. Governments today face the prospect of losing a cyberconflict without ever knowing the identity of their adversary.

Nation-states endeavor to retain as much control as they can over international conflict. However, globalization and the Internet have considerably strengthened the ability of anyone to follow current events, as well as the power to shape them. Transnational subcultures now spontaneously coalesce online, and influence myriad political agendas, without reporting to any chain of command. A challenge for national security leadership is whether such activity could spin delicate diplomacy out of control.

The Dangers to Electronic Infrastructures

Increasingly, governments around the world complain publicly of cyberespionage. On a daily basis, anonymous computer hackers secretly and illegally copy vast quantities of computer data and network communications. Theoretically, it is possible to conduct devastating intelligence gathering operations, even on highly sensitive political and military communications, remotely from anywhere in the world.

Cheap and effective, propaganda is often both the easiest and the most powerful cyberattack. Digital information, in text or image format—and regardless of whether it is true—can be instantly copied and sent anywhere in the world, even deep behind enemy lines. And provocative information that is removed from the Web may appear on another Web site in seconds.

Theoretically, it is possible to conduct devastating intelligence gathering operations, even on highly sensitive political and military communications, remotely from anywhere in the world.

The simple strategy behind a DoS [denial-of-service] attack is to deny the use of a computer resource to legitimate users. The most common tactic is to flood the target with so much superfluous data that it cannot respond to real requests for services or information. Other DoS attacks include physical destruction of computer hardware and the use of electromagnetic interference, designed to destroy unshielded electronics via current or voltage surges.

Data modification is extremely dangerous, because a successful attack can mean that legitimate users (human or machine) will make an important decision(s) based on maliciously altered information. Such attacks range from Web site defacement (often referred to as "electronic graffiti," but which can still carry propaganda or disinformation) to database attacks intended to corrupt weapons or command and control (C2) systems.

National critical infrastructures are, like everything else, increasingly connected to the Internet. However, because instant response is often required, and because associated hardware may have insufficient computing resources, security may not be robust. The management of electricity may be especially important for national security planners to evaluate, because electricity has no substitute, and all other infrastructures depend on it. Finally, it is important to note that almost all critical infrastructures are in private hands.

Russia and Chechnya Set the Example for Internet Propaganda

In the Internet era, unedited news from a war front can arrive in real time. Internet users worldwide play an important role in international conflicts simply by posting information, in either text or image format, to a Web site.

Since the earliest days of the World Wide Web, pro-Chechen and pro-Russian forces have waged a virtual war on the Internet, simultaneous to their conflict on the ground. The Chechen separatist movement in particular is considered a pioneer in the use of the Web as a tool for delivering powerful public relations messages. The skillful placement of propaganda and other information, such as the number to a war funds bank account in Sacramento, California, helped to unite the Chechen diaspora [the dispersion of people from their homeland].

The most effective information, however, was not pro-Chechen, but anti-Russian. Digital images of bloody corpses served to turn public opinion against perceived Russian military excesses. In 1999, just as Kremlin [Russian government] officials were denying an incident in which a Chechen bus was attacked and many passengers killed, images of the incident appeared on the Web. As technology progressed, Internet surfers watched streaming videos of favorable Chechen military activity, such as ambushes on Russian military convoys.

The Russian government admitted the need to improve its tactics in cyberspace. In 1999, Vladimir Putin, then Russia's prime minister, stated that "we surrendered this terrain some time ago . . . but now we are entering the game again." Moscow sought the help of the West in shutting down the important pro-Chechen Kavkaz.org Web site, and "the introduction of centralized military censorship regarding the war in the North Caucasus" was announced.

During the second Chechen war (1999–2000), Russian officials were accused of escalating the cyberconflict, by hacking into Chechen Web sites. The timing and sophistication of at least some of the attacks suggested nation-state involvement. For example, Kavkaz.org (hosted in the U.S.) was reportedly knocked off-line simultaneous to the storming by Russian special forces of a Moscow theater under siege by Chechen terrorists.

In 1999, just as Kremlin officials were denying an incident in which a Chechen bus was attacked and many passengers killed, images of the incident appeared on the Web.

The 1999 Birth of Cyberwar

In globalized, Internet-era conflicts, anyone with a computer and a connection to the Internet is a potential combatant. NATO's [North Atlantic Treaty Organization's] first major military engagement followed the explosive growth of the Web during the 1990s. Just as Vietnam was the world's first TV war, Kosovo was its first broadscale Internet war.

As NATO planes began to bomb Serbia, numerous pro-Serbian (or anti-Western) hacker groups, such as the Black Hand, began to attack NATO Internet infrastructure. It is unknown whether any of the hackers worked directly for the Yugoslav military; regardless, their stated goal was to disrupt NATO's military operations.

The Black Hand, which borrowed its name from the Pan-Slavic secret society that helped to start World War I, claimed it could enumerate NATO's "most important" computers, and that through hacking it would attempt to "delete all the data" on them. The group claimed success on at least one U.S. Navy computer, and stated that it was subsequently taken off-line.

NATO, U.S., and U.K. [United Kingdom] computers were all attacked during the war, via denial-of-service and virus-infected e-mail (25 different strains of viruses were detected). In the U.S., the White House Web site was defaced, and a Secret Service investigation ensued. While the U.S. claimed to have suffered "no impact" on the overall war effort, the UK admitted to having lost at least some database information.

At NATO headquarters in Belgium, the attacks were a public relations and propaganda victory for the hackers. The NATO public affairs Web site for the war in Kosovo, where the organization sought to portray its side of the conflict via briefings and news updates, was "virtually inoperable for several days." NATO spokesman Jamie Shea blamed "line saturation" on "hackers in Belgrade." A simultaneous flood of e-mail successfully choked NATO's e-mail server. As the organization endeavored to upgrade nearly all of its computer servers, the network attacks, which initially started in Belgrade, began to emanate from all over the world.

Cyberwarfare Now Accompanies Ground Conflict

During the Cold War, the Middle East often served as a proving ground for military weapons and tactics. In the Internet era, it has done the same for cyberwarfare.

In October 2000, following the abduction of three Israeli soldiers, blue and white flags and a sound file playing the Israeli national anthem were planted on a hacked Hizballah Web site. Subsequent pro-Israeli attacks targeted the official

---

Cyberwarfare Is Difficult to Define

Analysts and strategists gathered at the Cyber Warfare 2009 conference in London ... were grappling with some thorny problems associated with the cyberaggression threat. One that proved particularly vexing was the matter of exactly what constitutes cyberwarfare under international law. There's no global agreement on the definitions of cyberwarfare or cyberterrorism, so how does a nation conform to the rule of law if it's compelled to respond to a cyberattack? ...

Those definitions are especially elusive when you consider that no one can even be sure who the potential combatants are.

"There is some real work that needs to be done, not only in the U.S., but globally, to think about what is a use of force or an act of war in cyberspace," says Paul Kurtz, a partner at Good Harbor Consulting, LLC in Arlington, Virginia, and a former senior director for critical infrastructure protection on the White House's Homeland Security Council.

The need to establish global norms about what is acceptable behavior in cyberspace, he says, is complicated by the fact that "the weapons are not just in the hands of nation-states. They're essentially in everybody's hands."

Don Tennant, "The Fog of (Cyber) War," ComputerWorld.com, April 27, 2009.

Web sites of military and political organizations perceived hostile to Israel, including the Palestinian National Authority, Hamas, and Iran.

Retaliation from pro-Palestinian hackers was quick, and much more diverse in scope. Israeli political, military, telecommunications, media, and universities were all hit, and the attackers also targeted sites of pure economic value, including the Bank of Israel, e-commerce sites, and the Tel Aviv Stock Exchange. At the time, Israel was more wired to the Internet than all of its neighbors combined, so there was no shortage of targets. The *.il* country domain provided a well-defined list that pro-Palestinian hackers worked through methodically.

Wars often showcase new tools and tactics. During this conflict, the "Defend" DoS program was used to great effect by both sides, demonstrating in part that software can be copied more quickly than a tank or a rifle. Defend's innovation was to continually revise the date and time of its mock Web requests; this served to defeat the Web caching security mechanisms of the time.

The Middle East cyberwar demonstrated that Internet-era political conflicts quickly become internationalized. For example, the Pakistan Hackerz Club penetrated the U.S.-based pro-Israel lobby AIPAC [American Israel Public Affairs Committee], and published sensitive e-mails, credit card numbers, and contact information for some of its members, and the telecommunications firm AT&T was targeted for providing technical support to the Israeli government during the crisis.

Since 2000, the Middle East cyberwar has generally followed the conflict on the ground. In 2006, as tensions rose between Israel and Gaza, pro-Palestinian hackers shut down around 700 Israeli Internet domains, including those of Bank Hapoalim, Bank Otsar Ha-Hayal, BMW Israel, Subaru Israel, and McDonalds Israel.

The United States and China Engage in Patriotic Hacking

On April 26, 2001, the Federal Bureau of Investigation's (FBI's) National Infrastructure Protection Center (NIPC) released advisory 01009:

Citing recent events between the United States and the People's Republic of China (PRC), malicious hackers have escalated Web page defacements over the Internet. This communication is to advise network administrators of the potential for increased hacker activity directed at U.S. systems. . . . Chinese hackers have publicly discussed increasing their activity during this period, which coincides with dates of historic significance in the PRC.

Tensions had risen sharply between the two countries following the U.S. bombing of the Chinese embassy in Belgrade in 1999, and after the midair collision of a U.S. Navy plane with a Chinese fighter jet over the South China Sea in 2001, followed by the prolonged detainment of the American crew in the PRC.

Hackers on both sides of the Pacific, such as China Eagle Alliance [International] and Poizon B0x, began wide-scale Web site defacement, and built hacker portals with titles such as "USA Kill" and "China Killer." When the cyber skirmishes were over, both sides claimed defacements and DoSs in the thousands.

The FBI investigated a Honker Union of China (HUC), 17-day hack of a California electric power grid test network that began on April 25th. The case was widely dismissed as media hype at the time, but the CIA [Central Intelligence Agency] informed industry leaders in 2007 that not only is a tangible hacker threat to such critical infrastructure possible, it in fact has already happened.

On the anniversary of this cyberwar, as businesses were bracing for another round of hacking, the Chinese government is said to have successfully called for a stand-down at the last minute, suggesting that Chinese hackers may share a greater degree of coordination than their American counterparts.

A Curious Case of Cyberattacks in Estonia

On April 26, 2007, the Estonian government moved a Soviet World War II memorial out of the center of its capital, Tallinn, in a move that inflamed public opinion both in Russia and among Estonia's Russian minority population.

Beginning on April 27, Estonian government, law enforcement, banking, media, and Internet infrastructure endured three weeks of cyberattacks, whose impact still generates immense interest from governments around the world.

Because Estonians conduct over 98 percent of their banking online, the impact of multiple distributed denial-of-service (DDoS) attacks, that severed all communications to the country's two largest banks for up to two hours and rendered international services partially unavailable for days at a time, is obvious.

Less widely discussed, but likely of greater consequence— both to national security planners and to computer network defense personnel—were the Internet infrastructure (router) attacks on one of the Estonian government's ISPs [Internet service providers], which are said to have disrupted government communications for at least a "short" period of time.

On the propaganda front, a hacker defaced the Estonian prime minister's political party Web site on April 27, changing the home page text to a fabricated government apology for having moved the statue, along with a promise to move it back to its original location.

All political and military conflicts now have a cyber dimension, whose size and impact are difficult to predict. Attackers have at their disposal a wide variety of effective cyberwarfare strategies and tactics.

Diplomatic interest in this cyberattack was high in part due to the possible reinterpretation of NATO's Article 5, which states that "an armed attack against one [alliance member] shall be considered an attack against them all." Article 5 has been invoked only once, following the terrorist attacks of September 11, 2001. Potentially, it could one day be interpreted to encompass cyberattacks as well.

Critical Questions for National Security

All political and military conflicts now have a cyber dimension, whose size and impact are difficult to predict. Attackers have at their disposal a wide variety of effective cyberwarfare strategies and tactics.

Above all, the Internet is vulnerable to attack. Further, its amplifying power means that future victories in cyberspace could translate into victories on the ground. Both state and non-state actors enjoy a high return on investment in cyber tactics, which range from the placement of carefully crafted propaganda to the manipulation of an adversary's critical infrastructure. . . .

The Internet is changing much of life as we know it, to include the nature and conduct of warfare. At times, cyber tools and tactics will favor nations robust in information technology, but the Internet is a prodigious tool for a weaker party to attack a stronger conventional foe. As with terrorism and weapons of mass destruction, the dynamic, asymmetric, and still-evolving nature of cyberattacks makes all aspects of cyberdefense—including detection, analysis, investigation, prosecution, retaliation, and more—critical questions for national security planners to answer.

Cyberwar Is an Exaggeration

Evgeny Morozov

According to information technology expert Evgeny Morozov, reports of cyberwar, as well as the notion that coordinated attacks can bring down a major country's communication network, are overstated. Often these notions are promulgated by companies that provide computer security and have a financial interest in suggesting future cataclysmic attacks, Morozov argues in the following viewpoint. Despite attacks, reputedly by Russia, on Estonia and Georgia, no Internet doomsday scenario seems imminent. Instead of indulging in hyperbole by calling such attacks warfare, he asserts, countries need to invest more heavily in their Internet infrastructure to ward off cyberattacks.

Morozov, a native of Belarus, has served as a fellow at the Open Society Institute in New York and is working on a book about the Internet's role in authoritarian societies. He has also served as director of new media at the Prague-based organization Transitions Online and a columnist for the Russian newspaper Akzia.

As you read, consider the following questions:

1. According to Morozov, what major corporations have formed new business units to capitalize on cybersecurity?
2. What is a denial-of-service attack, in the author's view?

3. According to Morozov, why were the dangers from the Chinese "GhostNet" spying case overexaggerated?

The age of cyberwarfare has arrived. That, at any rate, is the message we are now hearing from a broad range of journalists, policy analysts, and government officials. Introducing a comprehensive White House report on cybersecurity released at the end of May [2009], President [Barack] Obama called cybersecurity "one of the most serious economic and national security challenges we face as a nation." His words echo a flurry of gloomy think tank reports. The Defense Science Board, a federal advisory group, recently warned that "cyberwarfare is here to stay," and that it will "encompass not only military attacks, but also civilian commercial systems." And "Securing Cyberspace for the 44th President," prepared by the Center for Strategic and International Studies, suggests that cybersecurity is as great a concern as "weapons of mass destruction or global jihad."

More Fears than Facts

Unfortunately, these reports are usually richer in vivid metaphor—with fears of "digital Pearl Harbors" and "cyber-Katrinas"—than in factual foundation.

Consider a frequently quoted CIA [Central Intelligence Agency] claim about using the Internet to cause widespread power outages. It derives from a public presentation by a senior CIA cybersecurity analyst in early 2008. Here is what he said:

> We have information, from multiple regions outside the United States, of cyberintrusions into utilities, followed by extortion demands. We suspect, but cannot confirm, that some of these attackers had the benefit of inside knowledge. We have information that cyberattacks have been used to disrupt power equipment in several regions outside the United States. In at least one case, the disruption caused a

power outage affecting multiple cities. We do not know who executed these attacks or why, but all involved intrusions through the Internet.

Reports are usually richer in vivid metaphor—with fears of 'digital Pearl Harbors' and 'cyber-Katrinas'—than in factual foundation.

So "there is information" that cyberattacks "have been used." When? Why? By whom? And have the attacks caused any power outages? The CIA may have some classified information, but very little that is unclassified suggests that such cyberintrusions have occurred.

Or consider an April 2009 *Wall Street Journal* article entitled "Electricity Grid in U.S. Penetrated by Spies." The article quotes no attributable sources for its starkest claims about cyberspying, names no utility companies as victims of intrusions, and mentions just one real cyberattack, which occurred in Australia in 2000 and was conducted by a disgruntled employee rather than an external hacker.

It is alarming that so many people have accepted the White House's assertions about cybersecurity as a key national security problem without demanding further evidence. Have we learned nothing from the WMD [weapons of mass destruction] debacle? The administration's claims could lead to policies with serious, long-term, troubling consequences for network openness and personal privacy.

Cybersecurity fears have had, it should be said, one unambiguous effect: They have fueled a growing cybersecurity market, which, according to some projections, will grow twice as fast as the rest of the IT [information technology] industry. Boeing, Raytheon, and Lockheed Martin, among others, have formed new business units to tap increased spending to protect U.S. government computers from cyberattacks. Moreover, many former government officials have made smooth transitions from national cybersecurity policy to the lucrative worlds of consulting and punditry. Speaking at a recent conference in Washington, D.C., Amit Yoran—a former cybersecurity czar in the [George W.] Bush administration and currently the CEO [chief executive officer] of NetWitness, a cybersecurity start-up—has called hacking a national security threat, adding that "cyber-9/11 has happened over the last ten years, but it's happened slowly, so we don't see it." One way for the government to protect itself from this cyber-9/11 [referring to 2001 terrorist attacks on the United States] may be to purchase NetWitness's numerous software applications, aimed at addressing both "state and non-state sponsored cyberthreats." . . .

Denial-of-Service Attacks

The ultimate doomsday scenario—think [of the Bruce Willis movie] *Live Free or Die Hard*—could involve a simultaneous attack on economic e-infrastructure and e-communications: Imagine al Qaeda disabling banks, destroying financial data, disrupting networks, and driving the American economy back to the nineteenth century. This certainly sounds scary—almost as scary as raptors in Central Park or a giant asteroid heading toward the White House. The latter two are not, however, being presented as "national security risks" yet.

There are certainly genuine security concerns associated with the Internet. But before accepting the demands of government agencies for new and increased powers to fight threats in cyberspace and prepare for cyberwarfare, we should look more closely at well-defined dangers and ask just where existing technological means and legal norms fall short. Because the technologies are changing so quickly, we cannot expect definitive answers. But cyberskeptics—who argue that cyberwarfare is still more of an urban legend than a credible hazard—appear to be onto something important.

One kind of cybersecurity problem grows out of resource scarcity. A network has only so much bandwidth; a server can serve only so much data at one time. So if you want to disable (or simply slow down) the computer backbone of a national economy, for example, you need to figure out how to reach its upper limit.

Cyberskeptics—who argue that cyberwarfare is still more of an urban legend than a credible hazard—appear to be onto something important.

It would be relatively easy to protect against this problem if you could cut your computer or network off from the rest of the world. But as the majority of governmental and commercial services have moved online, we expect them to be offered anywhere; Americans still want to access their online banking accounts at Chase even if they are travelling in Africa or Asia. What this means in practice is that institutions typically cannot shut off access to their online services based on nationality of the user or the origin of the computer (and in the case of news or entertainment sites, they do not want to: greater access means more advertising income).

Together, these limitations create an opportunity for attackers. Since no one, not even the U.S. government, has infinite computer resources, any network is potentially at risk.

Taking advantage of this resource scarcity could be an effective way of causing trouble for sites one does not like. The simplest—and also the least effective—way of doing this is to visit the URL and hit the "reload" button on your browser as often (and for as long) as you can. Congratulations: You have just participated in the most basic kind of "denial-of-service" (DoS) attack, which aims to deny or delay the delivery of online services to legitimate users. These days, however, it would be very hard to find a site that would suffer any noticeable damage from such a nuisance; what is missing from your cyberguerilla campaign is scale.

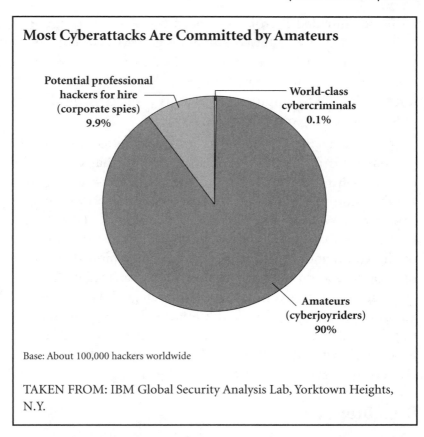

Most Cyberattacks Are Committed by Amateurs

Potential professional hackers for hire (corporate spies) 9.9%

World-class cybercriminals 0.1%

Amateurs (cyberjoyriders) 90%

Base: About 100,000 hackers worldwide

TAKEN FROM: IBM Global Security Analysis Lab, Yorktown Heights, N.Y.

Now multiply your efforts by a million—distribute your attacks among millions of other computers—and this could be enough to cause headaches to the administrators of many Web sites. These types of attacks are known as "distributed denial-of-service" or DDoS attacks. Administrators may be able to increase their traffic and bandwidth estimates and allocate more resources. Otherwise they have to live with this harassment, which may disable their Web site for long periods.

DDoS attacks work, then, by making heavier-than-normal demands on the underlying infrastructure, and they usually cause inconvenience rather than serious harm. . . .

In fact, your own computer may well be participating in a DDoS attack right now. You may, for example, have inadvertently downloaded a trojan—a hard-to-detect, tiny piece of software—that has allowed someone else to take control of your machine, without obvious effect on your computer's speed or operations. Some computer experts put the upper limit of infected computers as high as a quarter of all computers connected to the Internet.

Because a single computer is inconsequential, the infected computers form "botnets"—nets of robots—that can receive directions from a command-and-control center—usually just another computer on the network with the power to give commands. What makes the latest generation of botnets hard to defeat is that every infected computer can assume the role of the command-and-control center: Old-fashioned methods of decapitation do not work against such dispersed command-and-control. Moreover, botnets are strategic: When network administrators try to block the attacks, botnets can shift to unprotected prey. Commercial cybersecurity firms are trying to keep up with the changing threats; thus far, however, the botnets are staying at least one step ahead. . . .

Data Breaches

The security threats from DDoS attacks pale in comparison with the *potential* consequences of another kind of online insecurity, one more likely to be associated with terrorists than criminals and potentially more consequential politically: data breaches or network security compromises (I say "potential" because very few analysts with access to intelligence information agree to speak on the record). After all, with DDoS, attackers simply slow down *everyone's* access to data that are, in most cases, already public (some data are occasionally destroyed). With data breaches, in contrast, attackers can gain access to private and classified data, and with network security compromises, they might also obtain full control of high-value services like civil-aviation communication systems or nuclear reactors.

Data breaches and network security compromises also create far more exciting popular narratives: The media frenzy that followed the detection of China-based GhostNet—a large cyberspying operation that spanned more than 1,250 computers in 103 countries, many of them belonging to governments, militaries, and international organizations—is illustrative. Much like botnets, cyberspying operations such as GhostNet rely on inadvertently downloaded trojans to obtain full control over the infected computer. In GhostNet's case, hackers even gained the ability to turn on computers' camera and audio-recording functions for the purposes of remote surveillance, though we have no evidence that attackers used this function.

In fact, what may be most remarkable about GhostNet is what did *not* happen. No computers belonging to the U.S. or U.K. [United Kingdom] governments—both deeply concerned about cybersecurity—were affected; one NATO [North Atlantic Treaty Organization] computer was affected, but had no classified information on it. It might be unnerving that the computers in the foreign ministries of Brunei, Barbados, and Bhutan were compromised, but the cybersecurity standards and procedures of those countries probably are not at the global cutting edge. With some assistance on upgrades, they could be made much more secure.

In part, then, the solution to cyberinsecurity is simple: If you have a lot of classified information on a computer and do not want to become part of another GhostNet-like operation, do not connect it to the Internet. This is by far the safest way to preserve the integrity of your data. Of course, it may be impossible to keep your computer disconnected from *all* networks. And by connecting to virtually any network—no matter how secure—you relinquish sole control over your computer. In most cases, however, this is a tolerable risk: On average, you are better off connected, and you can guard certain portions of a network, while leaving others exposed. This is Network Security 101, and high-value networks are built by very smart IT experts. Moreover, most really sensitive networks are designed in ways that prevent third-party visitors— even if they manage somehow to penetrate the system—from doing much damage. For example, hackers who invade the e-mail system of a nuclear reactor will not be able to blow up nuclear facilities with a mouse click. Data and security breaches vary in degree, but such subtlety is usually lost on decision makers and journalists alike.

Although there is a continuous spectrum of attacks, running from classified memos to nuclear buttons, we have seen no evidence that access to the latter is very likely or even possible.

Exaggerated Problems

Hype aside, what we do know is that there are countless attacks on government computers in virtually every major Western country, many of them for the purpose of espionage and intelligence gathering; data have been lost, compromised, and altered. The United States may have been affected the most: The State Department estimates that it has lost "terabytes" of data to cyberattacks, while Pentagon press releases suggest that it is under virtually constant cybersiege. Dangerous as they are, these are still disturbing incidents of data loss rather than seriously breached data or compromised networks. Breakthroughs in encryption techniques have also made data more secure than ever. As for the data loss, the best strategy is to follow some obvious rules: Be careful, and avoid trafficking data in open spaces. (Don't put important data anywhere on the Internet, and don't leave laptops with classified information in hotel rooms.)

Although there is a continuous spectrum of attacks, running from classified memos to nuclear buttons, we have seen no evidence that access to the latter is very likely or even possible. Vigilance is vital, but exaggeration and blind acceptance of speculative assertions are not.

So why is there so much concern about "cyberterrorism"? Answering a question with a question: Who frames the debate? Much of the data are gathered by ultra-secretive government agencies—which need to justify their own existence—and cybersecurity companies—which derive commercial benefits from popular anxiety. Journalists do not help. Gloomy scenarios and speculations about cyber-Armaggedon draw attention, even if they are relatively short on facts.

Politicians, too, deserve some blame, as they are usually quick to draw parallels between cyberterrorism and conventional terrorism—often for geopolitical convenience—while glossing over the vast differences that make military metaphors inappropriate. In particular, cyberterrorism is anonymous, decentralized, and even more detached than ordinary terrorism from physical locations. Cyberterrorists do not need to hide in caves or failed states; "cybersquads" typically reside in multiple geographic locations, which tend to be urban and well-connected to the global communications grid. Some might still argue that state sponsorship (or mere toleration) of cyberterrorism could be treated as *casus belli* [an act of war], but we are yet to see a significant instance of cyberterrorists colluding with governments. All of this makes talk of large-scale retaliation impractical, if not irresponsible, but also understandable if one is trying to attract attention.

Gloomy scenarios and speculations about cyber-Armaggedon draw attention, even if they are relatively short on facts.

Attacks on Estonia and Georgia

Much of the cybersecurity problem, then, seems to be exaggerated: The economy is not about to be brought down, data and networks can be secured, and terrorists do not have the upper hand. But what about genuine cyberwarfare? The cyber-attacks on Estonia [a Baltic country] in April–May 2007 (triggered by squabbling between Tallinn and Moscow over the relocation of a Soviet-era monument) and the cyberdimension of the August 2008 war between Russia and [the former Soviet republic of] Georgia have reignited older debates about how cyberattacks could be used by and against governments.

The Estonian case is notable for the duration of the attacks—the country was under "DDoS-terror" for almost a month, with much of its crucial national infrastructure (including online banking) temporarily unavailable. The local media and some Estonian politicians were quick to blame the attacks on Russia, but no conclusive evidence emerged to prove this. The Georgian case—widely discussed as the first major instance of cyberattacks (primarily DDoS) accompanying conventional warfare—has barely lived up to its hype. Many Georgian government Web sites were, in fact, targets of severe DDoS attacks. So was at least one bank. Yet, the broader strategic importance of such attacks within the Russian military operation is not clear at all, nor did Russia acknowledge responsibility for the attacks.

Although the attacks on Estonia and Georgia are often grouped together—perhaps because of the tentative Russian involvement in both—they are also very different. One important difference is in the degree of technological sophistication of the two countries. Attacking the Internet in Estonia, which made Internet access a basic human right in 2000, is like attacking the banks in Lichtenstein [small German-speaking country]: The country's economy, politics, and even some emergency services are pegged to it so tightly that being offline is a national calamity.

Georgia, on the other hand, is a technological laggard. When Georgia's major government Web sites became inaccessible during the war, the Foreign Ministry was slow in finding a temporary home on a blog. The lapse may have gone largely unnoticed: 2006 Internet statistics gathered by the United Nations show that Georgia had about seven Internet users per one hundred population compared to 55 in Estonia and 70 in the United States. The Georgian case also highlights the danger of drawing too many strategic lessons from cyberattacks. After all, one common result of the loss of Internet access is power outages, common during wartime regardless of cyberattacks.

The United States may be able to forego dramatic and costly changes in favor of regular maintenance and incremental improvements.

Moreover, both Georgia and Estonia are in a sense "cyberlocked," with limited points of connection (even in Estonia) to the external Internet. This limited connectivity and the two country's dependence on physical infrastructure heighten their vulnerability. Less cyberlocked nations do not face the same risk. As Scott Pinzon, former information security analyst with WatchGuard Technologies, told me, "If Georgia or Estonia were enmeshed into the Internet as thoroughly as, say, the state of California, the cyberattacks against them would have been reduced to the level of nuisance." The smartest way to guard against future attacks may, then, be to build robust infrastructure—laying extra cables, creating more Internet exchange points (where Internet service providers share data), providing incentives for new Internet service providers, and attracting more players to sell connectivity in places that now have limited infrastructure. The United States has actually done quite a bit of this already, so the Estonian experience may have little to teach Americans. While it might benefit Estonia and some other countries to invest heavily in upgrades, the United States may be able to forego dramatic and costly changes in favor of regular maintenance and incremental improvements. . . .

Using the metrics of conventional conflicts to assess these attacks is not easy. How severe must the damage be in order for the cyberattacks to qualify as armed attacks?

For largely geopolitical reasons, Estonia initially called the cyberattacks a cyberwar, a move that now seems ill-considered (on a recent trip to Estonia, I noticed that Estonian officials had replaced the term "cyberwar" with the more neutral "cyberattacks"). The militarization of cyberspace that inevitably comes with any talk of war is disturbing, for there is no evidence yet to link the current generation of cyberattacks to warfare, at least not in the legal sense of the term. . . .

Simple Solutions

Putting these complexities aside and focusing just on states, it is important to bear in mind that the cyberattacks on Estonia and especially Georgia did little damage, particularly when compared to the physical destruction caused by angry mobs in the former and troops in the latter. One argument about the Georgian case is that cyberattacks played a strategic role by thwarting Georgia's ability to communicate with the rest of the world and present its case to the international community. This argument both overestimates the Georgian government's reliance on the Internet and underestimates how much international PR [public relations]—particularly during wartime—is done by lobbyists and publicity firms based in Washington, Brussels, and London. There is, probably, an argument to be made about the vast psychological effects of cyberattacks—particularly those that disrupt ordinary economic life. But there is a line between causing inconvenience and causing human suffering, and cyberattacks have not crossed it yet.

The usefulness of cyberattacks as a military tool is also contested. Some experts are justifiably skeptical about the arrival of a new age of cyberwar. Marcus J. Ranum, chief security officer of Tenable Network Security, argues that it is pointless for superpowers to develop cyberwar capabilities to attack non-superpowers, as they can crush them in more conventional ways. As for non-superpowers, their use of cybercapabilities would almost certainly result in what Ranum calls "the blind Mike Tyson" effect [after the former boxing champion]: The superpower would retaliate with off-line weaponry ("blind me, I nuke you"). If Ranum is right, we should forget about the prospect of all-out cyberwar until we have technologically advanced superpowers that are hostile to each other. Focusing on cybercrime, cyberterrorism, and cyberespionage may help us address the more pertinent threats in a more rational manner.

In the meantime, those truly concerned about the future of the Internet, global security, and e-Katrinas would be advised to watch a recent *South Park* [the animated situation comedy] episode, in which the Internet suddenly disappears and hordes of obsessed families head to the Internet Refugee Camp in California, where they are allowed to browse their favorite Web sites for 40 seconds a day, while the military fights the no-longer-blinking giant Internet router. Finally, a nine-year-old boy plugs the router back in, and its magic green light returns. This would make a sensible strategy for many governments, which are all too eager to adopt militaristic postures instead of focusing on making their own Internet infrastructures more robust.

Periodical Bibliography

The following articles have been selected to supplement the diverse views presented in this chapter.

Zakariyya Adaramola   "Nigeria: Yahoo Boys with Bankers' Help Return in Full Force," *Daily Trust*, September 6, 2008.

Esther Dyson   "The Internet's Immune System," Project Syndicate, March 19, 2009. www.project-syndicate.org.

Economist   "Cyberwar—Battle Is Joined," April 26, 2009.

Steven Furnell   "Cybercrime: The Transformation of Crime in the Information Age—By D.S. Wall," *British Journal of Sociology*, March 5, 2008.

O.B. Longe and S.C. Chiemeke   "Cyber Crime and Criminality in Nigeria—What Roles Are Internet Access Points Playing?" *European Journal of Social Sciences*, 2008.

Mike McConnell   "Cyberwar Is the New Atomic Age," *New Perspectives Quarterly*, Summer 2009.

New Scientist   "Fighting a Cyberwar: It's Less Bloody than Bombing, but a Cyberattack That Shuts Down a Hospital's Systems Could Kill Just as Effectively," 2008.

Michael Reilly   "How Long Before All-Out Cyberwar?" *New Scientist*, February 20, 2008.

Gene Stephens   "Cybercrime in the Year 2025," *Futurist*, July 2, 2008.

Gabriel Weimann and Katharina Von Knop   "Applying the Notion of Noise to Countering Online Terrorism," *Studies in Conflict & Terrorism*, October 2008.

Glossary

ARPANET an early computer network created by the U.S. Department of Defense

bandwidth the amount of information that can be sent through a particular Internet connection

blog a Web journal

browser software that enables a user to view and navigate around the World Wide Web

cybercrime any crime related to computing or the Internet

cyberspace the entire range of information that is available on the Internet

cyberterrorism terrorist activities facilitated by computers or the Internet

cyberwar when one country attempts to attack another's computer or networking capabilities

denial-of-service attack a form of cyberwar or cybercrime in which one party bombards a Web site with traffic so that legitimate users cannot access it

encryption to code information so that only someone with the ability to translate it can understand it

FAQ frequently asked questions

FTP file transfer protocol: a method of moving information between computers

HTML hypertext markup language: the code used to create Web documents

hyperlink a connection between information and Web sites on the World Wide Web

Internet the international computer network composed of numerous smaller networks linked together

ISP Internet service provider: companies that provide access to the Internet for individuals, businesses, and organizations

netizen slang for an Internet citizen or Internet user

podcasting broadcasting audio over the Internet

protocol the standard rules by which computers transmit and receive packets of information

server a computer that allows other computers to store or access information

TCP/IP transmission control protocol/Internet protocol: the set of rules that regulates information on the Internet and ensures that information reaches the proper destination

URL the Internet address of a Web site

VoIP voice over Internet protocol: a method of using the Internet for telephone service

World Wide Web all of the various Web sites on the Internet devoted to entities such as schools, governments, organizations, and individuals

For Further Discussion

Chapter 1

1. After reading the viewpoints in this chapter, do you believe the Internet is a wondrous invention or a technological scourge? Explain your answer.

2. After reading the viewpoint by Ariana Eunjung Cha, do you think Internet addiction should be considered in a category by itself, or does it merely facilitate traditional harmful addictions such as gambling and pornography?

3. In your opinion, will the Internet destroy or promote threatened industries, such as journalism and music?

Chapter 2

1. After reading the viewpoints in this chapter, do you think the Internet will help politicians reach people in a new way or will the Internet simply promote the same abuses, such as negative campaigning, already present in traditional media?

2. According to the viewpoints in this chapter, how has the Internet facilitated democracy around the world and how has it been used to impede democratic progress?

Chapter 3

1. How, according to the viewpoints in this chapter, do repressive regimes use Internet censorship to control their citizens?

2. In your opinion, should the Internet be kept "neutral" so that complete freedom on the Internet is ensured for all users, or must there be restrictions placed on usage for the good of society?

3. After reading the viewpoints in this chapter, discuss how Internet censorship and regulation sometimes create more problems than they solve.

Chapter 4

1. According to the articles by Zakariyya Adaramola, Rob Sharp, and Lynne Roberts, what are some methods criminals use to prey on online victims?

2. Do the viewpoints in this chapter convince you that authorities are doing enough to combat Internet crime, or does it seem that such crimes need more attention?

3. Is cyberwar a true threat to governments as Kenneth Geers argues, or is Evgeny Morozov correct in stating that it is not yet a legitimate tactic?

Organizations to Contact

The editors have compiled the following list of organizations concerned with the issues debated in this book. The descriptions are derived from materials provided by the organizations. All have publications or information available for interested readers. The list was compiled on the date of publication of the present volume; the information provided here may change. Be aware that many organizations take several weeks or longer to respond to inquiries, so allow as much time as possible.

Association Electronique Libre (AEL)
rue de Leumont 36, Wanze   B4520
  Belgium
Web site: www.ael.be

The Association Electronique Libre is a Belgian association protecting the fundamental rights in the information society. The AEL supports the freedoms of speech, press, and association on the Internet and any electronic media; the right to use encryption software for private communication; the right to write software unimpeded by private monopolies; and the right to access and preserve public domain and free digital information. Articles on Internet issues involving human rights and civil liberties are available on its Web site.

Berkman Center for Internet and Society
23 Everett Street, 2nd Floor, Cambridge, MA   02138
(617) 495-7547 • fax: (617) 495-7641
e-mail: cyber@law.harvard.edu
Web site: http://cyber.law.harvard.edu/

The Berkman Center for Internet and Society's mission is to explore and understand cyberspace; to study its development, dynamics, norms, and standards; and to assess the need or lack thereof for laws and sanctions. The Berkman Center is primarily research-oriented and is premised on the observation that what its researchers seek to learn is not already recorded. Publications on a wide variety of Web-related issues can be found on the center's Web site.

Electronic Frontier Foundation (EFF)

454 Shotwell Street, San Francisco, CA   94110-1914
(415) 436 9333 • fax: (415) 436 9993
e-mail: information@eff.org
Web site: www.eff.org

The Electronic Frontier Foundation is an organization that aims to foster a better understanding of civil liberties issues that arise from advancements in electronic communications. It supports litigation that preserves, protects, and extends First Amendment rights related to computers and telecommunications. Its annual reports are available on its Web site as well as white papers on cutting-edge technology issues and the e-mail newsletter, *Effector*.

Human Rights Watch

350 Fifth Avenue, 34th floor, New York, NY   10118-3299
(212) 290-4700 • fax: (212) 736-1300
e-mail: hrwnyc@hrw.org
Web site: www.hrw.org

Human Rights Watch is an independent, nongovernmental organization dedicated to protecting the human rights of people around the world. Human Rights Watch investigates and exposes human rights violations, including those limiting the freedom of expression. Human Rights Watch publishes numerous studies that are available on its Web site.

Internet Engineering Task Force (IETF)

IETF Secretariat, c/o Association Management Solutions LLC (AMS), 48377 Fremont Boulevard, Suite 117
Fremont, California   94538
(510) 492-4080 • fax: (510) 492-4001

e-mail: ietf-info@ietf.org
Web site: www.ietf.org

The Internet Engineering Task Force (IETF) is an open international community of network designers, operators, vendors, and researchers concerned with the evolution of Internet architecture and the smooth operation of the Internet. It is open to any interested individual. The actual technical work of the IETF is done in its working groups, which are organized by topic into several areas (e.g., routing, transport, security, etc.). News, publications, and links are available on its Web site.

Internet Society (ISOC)

1775 Wiehle Avenue, Suite 201, Reston, VA   20190-5108
(703) 439-2120 • fax: (703) 326-9881
e-mail: isoc@isoc.org
Web site: www.isoc.org

The Internet Society (ISOC) is a nonprofit organization founded in 1992 to provide leadership in Internet-related standards, education, and policy. The Internet Society is dedicated to ensuring the open development, evolution, and use of the Internet for the benefit of people throughout the world. The organization provides leadership in addressing issues that confront the future of the Internet and is the organizational home for the groups responsible for Internet infrastructure standards, including the Internet Engineering Task Force (IETF) and the Internet Architecture Board (IAB). The Internet Society acts not only as a global clearinghouse for Internet information and education, but also as a facilitator and coordinator of Internet-related initiatives around the world. It publishes the magazine *On the Internet.*

Privacy International (PI)

265 Strand, London   WC2R 1BH
    United Kingdom
+44.208.123.7933

e-mail: privacyint@privacy.org
Web site: www.privacyinternational.org

Privacy International (PI) is a human rights group formed in 1990 as a watchdog on surveillance and privacy invasions by governments and corporations. PI is based in London, England, and has an office in Washington, D.C. PI has campaigned across the world to protect people against intrusion by governments and corporations. PI's Web site features many documents, including reports, studies, and press releases that focus on Web privacy.

World Wide Web Consortium (W3C)
W3C/MIT, 32 Vassar Street, Room 32-G515
Cambridge, MA   02139
(617) 253-2613 • fax: (617) 258-5999
e-mail: team-liaisons@w3.org
Web site: www.w3.org

The mission of the World Wide Web Consortium (W3C) is to lead the World Wide Web to its full potential by developing protocols and guidelines that ensure its long-term growth. One of W3C's primary goals is to make these benefits available to all people, whatever their hardware, software, network infrastructure, native language, culture, geographical location, or physical or mental ability. W3C's vision for the Web involves participation, sharing knowledge, and building trust on a global scale. W3C supports the notion that the Web was invented as a communications tool intended to allow anyone, anywhere to share information. W3C standards have supported the evolution of the Web from a read-only tool to a complete communications vehicle. Articles and other information are available on its Web site.

Bibliography of Books

Stuart Allan — *Online News: Journalism and the Internet.* Maidenhead, England: Open University Press, 2006.

Scott Beattie — *Community, Space and Online Censorship: Regulating Pornotopia.* Surrey, England: Ashgate, 2009.

Birgit Beumers, Stephen C. Hutchings, and Natalia Rulyova, eds. — *The Post-Soviet Russian Media: Conflicting Signals.* London: Routledge, 2009.

Steven Branigan — *High-Tech Crimes Revealed: Cyberwar Stories from the Digital Front.* Boston, MA: Addison-Wesley, 2005.

Fernando Duarte Carvalho and Eduardo Mateus da Silva, eds. — *Cyberwar-Netwar: Security in the Information Age.* Amsterdam: IOS Press, in cooperation with the NATO Public Diplomacy Division, 2006.

Andrew Chadwick and Philip N. Howard, eds. — *Routledge Handbook of Internet Politics.* London: Routledge, 2009.

Jack L. Goldsmith and Tim Wu — *Who Controls the Internet? Illusions of a Borderless World.* New York: Oxford University Press, 2008.

Justin Healey, ed. — *Impacts of the Internet.* Thirroul, NSW: Spinney Press, 2006.

Human Rights Watch — *"Race to the Bottom": Corporate Complicity in Chinese Internet Censorship.* New York: Human Rights Watch, 2006.

Nicola F. Johnson — *The Multiplicities of Internet Addiction: The Misrecognition of Leisure and Learning.* Aldershot, England: Ashgate, 2009.

Athina Karatzogianni, ed. — *Cyber-Conflict and Global Politics.* Milton Park, Abingdon, Oxon, England: Routledge, 2009.

Lucy Küng, Robert G. Picard, and Ruth Towse, eds. — *The Internet and the Mass Media.* Los Angeles: SAGE, 2008.

Garrett Monaghan and Sean Tunney, eds. — *Web Journalism: A New Form of Citizenship?* Portland, OR: Sussex Academic Press, 2010.

Kathryn C. Montgomery — *Generation Digital: Politics, Commerce, and Childhood in the Age of the Internet.* Cambridge, MA: MIT Press, 2007.

Sarah Oates, Diana Owen, and Rachel K. Gibson, eds. — *The Internet and Politics: Citizens, Voters and Activists.* London: Routledge, 2006.

Jussi Parikka and Tony D. Sampson, eds. — *The Spam Book: On Viruses, Porn, and Other Anomalies from the Dark Side of Digital Culture.* Cresskill, NJ: Hampton Press, 2009.

Frank Schmalleger and Michael Pittaro, eds.
Crimes of the Internet. Upper Saddle River, NJ: Prentice Hall, 2009.

Kerry Sheldon and Dennis Howitt
Sex Offenders and the Internet. Chichester, England: John Wiley & Sons, 2007.

Daniel J. Solove
The Future of Reputation: Gossip, Rumor, and Privacy on the Internet. New Haven, CT: Yale University Press, 2007.

Corinne Sweet
Hooked on the Net: Internet Addiction—What It Is, How to Spot It and What to Do About It. London: Fusion, 2008.

Cristina Venegas
Digital Dilemmas: The State, the Individual, and Digital Media in Cuba. New Brunswick, NJ: Rutgers University Press, 2010.

Gabriel Weimann
Terror on the Internet: The New Arena, the New Challenges. Washington, DC: United States Institute of Peace Press, 2006.

Darrell M. West and Edward Alan Miller
Digital Medicine: Health Care in the Internet Era. Washington, DC: Brookings Institution Press, 2009.

Monica Whitty and Adam Joinson
Truth, Lies and Trust on the Internet. New York: Routledge, 2009.

Xiaoling Zhang and Yongnian Zheng, eds.

China's Information and Communications Technology Revolution: Social Changes and State Responses. London: Routledge, 2009.

Jonathan Zittrain

The Future of the Internet—and How to Stop It. New Haven, CT: Yale University Press, 2009.

Index

Geographic headings and page numbers in **boldface** refer to viewpoints about that country or region.